putting the pieces together

Help For Single Parents

Velma Thorne Carter
and
J. Lynn Leavenworth

Judson Press ® Valley Forge

The authors gratefully acknowledge the following persons:

Dr. Barbara Krasner, Margaret Cotroneo, and Dr. Douglas Schoeninger, who taught us new dimensions of human relationships and held us accountable;

Marie Richardson, who gave back more than we had given;

the hundreds of single parents who trusted us enough to share their pain.

V. T. C. and J. L. L.

PUTTING THE PIECES TOGETHER

Copyright © 1977
Judson Press, Valley Forge, PA 19481

Library of Congress Cataloging in Publication Data

Carter, Velma T
  Putting the pieces together.

  1. Single parent family. I. Leavenworth, Lynn, joint author. II. Title.
HQ734.C332   362.8'2   77-4085
ISBN 0-8170-0746-6

Photographs and illustrations by George H. Carter, Jr.

The name JUDSON PRESS is registered as a trademark in the U.S. Patent Office. Printed in the U.S.A. ⊕

to Marie and Harold

who gave support
when the ledgers of time
were unbalanced

The Chrysalis

The chrysalis is the intermediate stage in the life of a butterfly, in which its true self emerges. Having turned inward, it draws upon all of its resources and sets inexorably upon a journey outward. From here it emerges as a balanced and beautiful being.

preface

The life of the single parent has been described by some as "the land of beginning again." To an extent, that is true; there is the feeling of having been sent back to the starting gate. But it's more than that for most people. The pain of a broken relationship, the responsibility of children, the financial worry, the sense of having failed are among the burdens that accompany the starting again. The single parent struggles to survive while wading through a morass of grief and guilt, legal hassles, and property settlements. And worst of all—ALONE!

During the past five years, the authors have listened to hundreds of single parents retelling their experiences, sharing with others in a supportive educational group. The courage displayed by these people in the wake of their broken relationships convinced us that others could benefit by hearing about their struggles.

This book is not a survival manual for single parents. It is meant to help you to get some perspective on the situation in which you find yourself, to identify what your needs are, to direct you to some sources of help, and to encourage you to believe that life can have meaning and purpose in spite of all the problems that you are presently facing. We believe you are capable of more than simply "coping." We believe that your divorce or separation or the death of your spouse, traumatic as such an event may be, can have some very positive meaning for you. Whether you willed it or not, you have before you an opportunity to reassess, to retool on the basis of some new goals. While you cannot be both father and mother to your children, you can be *parent,* even if you don't have custody of them.

Once your grief has ended and you are able to close the door on your relationship with your former spouse, you will have to find your way back to the "singles' world" and face the challenge of new relationships and, possibly one day, remarriage.

We hope this book will instruct you, encourage you, and even inspire you. Most of all, we hope we can convince you that, indeed, *you are not alone!*

contents

a parable
of the trees

The forest is deep and quiet, and the only sounds that break the silence are made by the processes of life that allow the forest to renew itself: small animals and larger ones, each performing its appointed task, carrying seeds, controlling underbrush, struggling to survive the fierce competition required for nature's balance; the swaying of branches to cool the forest, to propel the seeds, and to give light and drink to all its forms of life.

A soft summer evening comes, and the cricket announces the temperature while a thrush trills a melody to the rising moon. Acorns fall from the great white oak and drop with a thudding rhythm on the ground beneath. A pair of cunning squirrels scamper quickly to retrieve the winter's bounty, carrying the acorns to their secret place nearby.

The seasons come and go—winter, spring, summer, and fall— and the rains and snows drop on the mounds of fallen leaves, pushing the acorns more firmly into the ground. The earth cradles the acorns, nourishing them until at last tiny branches reach out for light, small roots reach down into the soil, and two new oak trees are born.

Protected by the giant oak and by the community of life around them, the trees grow in strength and beauty as they reach higher and higher with each coming season. They bend easily in the storm, but their arms are strong. The trees, no longer infant growth, flower in youthful beauty, reach out, and touch. Their roots intertwine beneath the forest floor, anchoring each other, giving strength, receiving strength. Their branches dance together, dance away and back again.

Through months of aching cold and sweltering heat, they share whatever comes.

A new sound rises, at first a soft, repeating rhythm. Then growing, increasing, pounding, groaning. At last, through the dense forest, with ugly roar and offensive air, the machine appears beside the giant oak. The motor stops; and the single occupant climbs down, surveys the clustered trees, and then, with movements swift and sure, moves the young oak trees, testing their strength.

The intruder mounts his machine again, turns it around, and then, without further hesitation, scoops up the nearest member of the pair and with a roar moves on, carrying off the oak tree from its mate.

The earth lies open with a ragged wound. The roots of the remaining tree are exposed and torn, still clinging to the shorn-off roots of the other tree. The young oak, once firm and strong, struggles to remain upright. In the night a storm sweeps through the forest, and the tree shudders and wavers in the wind. Its roots clutch the soil, reaching deeper into the ground.

When morning comes, the oak still stands. The rain has washed the sky and pushed the warm earth around its broken roots. Healing begins, and the forest protects the tree. Slowly, then more rapidly, the branches of the oak reach up for sunlight, finding more room now that its partner is gone.

The branches of the oak spread protecting arms over the floor of the forest, providing shelter for another generation of its own. The leaves of the tree turn here, turn there, and with the coming of the wind begin to dance again.

10

you are
not alone

Don't let anyone tell you that you can't make it, because you can. Not only can you make it, but you can also come through the morass of problems and the personal suffering that divorce or separation or death has brought you; and you can do more than that. Provided that you are willing to face some hard issues, to call upon resources that are available to you both within yourself and without, and, finally, to fill your cup with determination; you'll not only make it, but you'll also find that life can move again, that you can laugh again, and that your spirit can dance once more.

11

A few years ago, we would have agreed with the distraught woman who cried out, "I can't go on; I've gone dead inside; I can't make it." But not now. Not any longer do we believe it can't be done, because we have seen too many single parents who have found their way through the maze of legal, financial, and personal difficulties; who have moved from despair to hope, from resignation to purpose, from grief to joy. We see them today, astonished at themselves, drawing on resources they didn't know they had, showing courage they had never needed, facing things they thought they could never face.

The actuarial tables frightened some of them into taking a stand. A forty-year-old woman said, "Oh, my God, you mean I've got forty more years to go—like this?" Her own answer was clear; "No—not like this." Then, turning to the counselor, she said,

I guess I've been kidding myself that at least some of these problems I'm facing will just go away if I don't look at them. I'm ready to do *something,* but there are so many problems that they overwhelm me, and I can't get started on any of them. I still love my husband, and I can't believe he's gone. I tell myself that if I had done this or that differently, he might not have left. Why couldn't we make it? What was the matter with us? My kids are falling apart, and, believe it or not, they take it out on me. I'm lonely, but my friends don't have time for my moaning. I feel as if I'm a fish out of water! And then, on top of it all are the bills—what in the world can I do about them? So here I am, wishing there were some kind of pill I could take for each one of those problems. Can you give me a prescription?

Unfortunately, there is no magic elixir that can wipe out the reality of all the things which that woman mentioned. Nor can anybody give you a prescription for instant joy. What we can do is to help you to sort out some of the alternatives you have, identify some of the hard issues that have to be faced, provide you with some new tools for doing what has to be done, and perhaps increase your courage to get on with the job.

The Pain of Separation

Separation hits hard when it comes. Whether it comes suddenly and unexpectedly or is the culmination of a growing knowledge of the inevitable, it hurts! I AM ALONE! And right on the heels of that shocking realization comes the double whammy: I AM STILL RESPONSIBLE FOR THESE CHILDREN!

12

That's not the way the story was supposed to go, you think. John and Mary were supposed to live "happily ever after" and raise their beautiful children and have a little cottage with a picket fence and a puppy and a kitten; and then they have grandchildren and walk together down a country lane toward the sunset. John wasn't supposed to die. OR Mary wasn't supposed to abandon me and the kids. I must be losing my mind—this cannot be happening to me.

It *can* be happening and *is* happening to you and to millions of others. Most of us cannot relate to numbers in the millions, for each of us has a set of circumstances in our relationships that is unique. The pain of a broken relationship is very real to each person involved, and each individual must then be able to own that pain and to be willing to ask for help in trying to heal the wounds which are the source of pain.

Nobody and no insight, however wise, can help the person who is unwilling or unable to help himself or herself. No one can do for you what you must do for yourself. The task is not easy, and you must be willing to pay the price of facing dealing with difficult issues.

There is more at stake here than merely coping with the present situation, as important as that is. We are talking about seizing the present as an opportunity to reassess your own values, your relationships, your experiences and abilities, and to take the first steps toward setting some clear and obtainable goals. In these processes you will find yourself reworking or reaffirming relationships that are important to you and moving toward an intentional life-style that can bring fulfillment to you and deep satisfaction in relationships with your children.

There are bound to be periods of greater pain than you are now experiencing; there may be times when the cost will seem to be more than you are willing to pay. But the assurance that you are moving in a direction you want to go will make it worth the cost.

Security

All of us like to have a feeling of security. We need to feel secure throughout our lives. We like to avoid pain. The Constitution guarantees the right at least to *pursue* happiness. All during our childhood we are conditioned to believe that we will grow up with a mother and father who love us, supply our needs, provide for our wants, and be available when we need them. We hope to be well liked by our peers, even to be envied by them, to fall in love with a wonderful mate, to marry, and eventually to have a home of our own in which children have the same expectations we ourselves have had. Nobody ever goes down the aisle without at least hoping to "live happily ever after."

13

"Ever after" has turned out to be a lot shorter than "ever" for a growing number in our society. Along came dissension, disillusionment, abandonment, unfaithfulness, or cruelty—or death—and the security of loving and being loved was suddenly gone.

We both knew that the marriage was dead. We were going separate ways for a long time before we were willing to admit that we were playing a game, keeping up appearances for the kids and our friends.

Neither of us thought it would be difficult to break up; in many ways, it would be a relief. But before we got through dividing up everything and turning our backs on what we had worked so hard for all those years, I was devastated. We had failed each other somehow, and now we were abandoning our commitment. Don't let anyone kid you; there's no such thing as painless separation.

Abandonment exacts its price in pain. The hurt may take

different forms, but it is there nevertheless. For example, Jack, married eight years, said:

> I'm really lonely. Our marriage was such a mess. I never came in the house that she didn't hit me with some accusation about what I did or didn't do. I'm just a naturally sloppy person, and she never got over expecting perfection. One day I realized I simply could not face that hassle another time, and I took off. I miss the kids so much; and though I see them occasionally, it is not the same. I have tried to work out some way that we could try again, but there is so much bitterness now that I know it would never work. Funny thing is, I thought it would be so easy for me.

Life settles into patterns that are familiar and comfortable; and when that pattern is broken, even deliberately, it can be very difficult. In our minds we conceive relationships in ways that make our own lives secure and tenable. When the structures that surround the relationships break, we find ourselves in an untenable position—not able to break away, yet not able to stay within the framework.

Coping with Change

The sudden change, the trauma of a broken relationship, can be extremely difficult; yet no matter how traumatic it is, people *do* survive change, and they do move forward. The ability to cope with change is a remarkable and recurring human attribute.

Every person has experienced sudden and dramatic changes in his or her life—in ways of living, in basic human relationships, in health status. For some, this kind of change is taken in stride, with the reaction being uneasiness, discomfort, or perhaps annoyance. For others, the reaction may be much more serious, producing extreme trauma related to acute anxiety.

What kinds of changes in your life have caused you to make serious readjustments in your life-style and were difficult for you to handle? Would your list read something like this?

First day of school
Moving to a new house
Going to summer camp
*   for the first time*
Starting high school
Death of a parent
Starting college

14

Marriage

Serious illness

Divorce

If you haven't already listed it, you will want to add to your list the most traumatic and difficult change that any human being ever experiences: birth. The mother's womb provides everything necessary to support life—food, warmth, security. The growing fetus is insulated from shock, is comfortable (even while making its mother most uncomfortable at times), and has nothing to do but prepare for the birth process. Then, suddenly, the shock of birth! This helpless, defenseless, totally dependent infant is propelled into a harsh and cruel environment. There is pain; there is innate fear.

Fortunately, the instinctive survival capacity sees the infant through the harshness that follows the separation from the mother's body. During the first hours following the separation, the child is passed from hand to hand as various experts do this or that. No matter how carefully and lovingly these necessary tasks are performed—or how warm, comfortable, and secure the little bed into which the infant is placed is—nevertheless, the infant is left, finally, alone. Abandoned! Yet the infant, except in rare instances, survives and grows. Because of the trauma of birth, the adventure of life can begin.

When the pain is too great—from hunger, discomfort, or fear— the infant communicates in the only language available—crying—to announce that help is needed. *The infant calls on the resources that are available to get relief from discomfort and pain.* The child cries— the response comes—the child begins to trust—the child gains strength and grows.

The analogy of the newborn child to your situation is obvious. The shock experienced in moving from the couples' to the singles' world requires a complete adjustment to new circumstances. You, too, must communicate your needs to sources of help. You probably will need some outside assistance to see you through to the point where you have learned to cope with your new situation.

You must crawl before you walk and walk before you run. So the first moves forward will be tentative ones—testing, trusting, growing.

Fear of the Unknown

New situations always bring concerns about the unknown,

especially if experience has taught us that we might get hurt in the process. We're unsure of our untested skills; we may not have confidence in ourselves because of damaged self-image. In these cases, we find a great many people who spend a lot of wasted energy "what-if-ing." What if one of the kids gets sick in the middle of the night? What if I have to go to work? What if I can't find someone to take care of the kids? What if . . . what if . . .? Even when those uncertainties are not about really important matters, they can pile up until the very bulk of them prevents a rational consideration of how to dispel the worry. One woman, the mother of three young children, told this story:

> The nights were the hardest. Not only was I lonely, I was just plain afraid to be alone in the house. I'd read until very late because I had no one to talk to, and everyone thought I was so self-sufficient. Sometimes I'd lie in the dark imagining all the terrible things that might happen with no other adult there. I had made my husband leave because I could no longer tolerate his alcoholism and abuse, and now I began to wonder if it wasn't better when he was there. At least I wasn't afraid of someone breaking in.

> One night I heard a noise in the kitchen. It sounded exactly as if a key were being fitted into the door. My heart was doing a double-time thump. I lay there, knowing I could not reach a phone without being seen from the outside and terrified of what might happen to the kids. Finally, I could stand it no longer, and I jumped out of bed and threw on the light switch. No one was there. After repeating this performance three or four times, I finally discovered a tiny mouse playing with a marble under the radiator near the door.

> My relief was so great and the situation so silly that I woke up my six-year-old to laugh with me.

When asked what gave her the strength to get up and investigate, the woman said, "Well, I knew that if there was someone at that door, it would be better to face them there than in the bedroom. And I knew that hiding under the covers wouldn't protect my children." She had coped.

Some fears are not so easily dispelled; some problems do not yield to quick solutions. Nor is coping what this book is all about. Coping is only the first step in your adjustment; and there is so much more, even though coping can be a victory in itself. Of course, it's tough to get on with the practical matters that press in on you, but it could be a serious mistake to believe that the practical things can be handled without concern for your own healing process.

There are two levels of response which you may need to make in your adjustment. One is to surmount the practical problems and get the management matters into some semblance of order; and the other is to give serious attention to the emotional wounds sustained by you and your children. When both of those have been attended to, you will be better prepared to begin looking to the future, toward an intentional life-style.

Let's begin, then, with a consideration of the resources you have available and to whom you may want to turn for help.

Available Resources

Anyone who has put a lot of effort and years into a marriage only to have it end is apt to feel that the loss of that investment has resulted in emotional bankruptcy. The loss can be an excuse for giving up, for never trying again, or it can be viewed as a time for reassessing and beginning the process of rebuilding.

We are going to assume that you at least want to try. If so, begin by assessing your resources. Think of them in these categories: personal, familial, fraternal, community, financial, and spiritual.

Personal resources

This may be the point at which you feel the greatest deficiency. Loss of self-image is common among persons who have lost a mate through either divorce or death. Many people have submerged their own personality so completely in that of their spouse that they have difficulty in feeling whole when the spouse is gone. Or if they have been rejected—made to feel inadequate by the mate's preference for someone else—they find it hard to feel any kind of self-worth. For example, one man, Paul, recounted his experience:

17

> We were married very young, and it lasted ten years. I thought we were very happy. We had two children right away, and they are beautiful kids. Marcia is a very attractive woman, and I loved her deeply. I had to be away from home occasionally; and, of course, it was hard for Marcia, especially while the kids were little. She took a job when the kids started school. That helped with our budget a lot, and I was happy about it. I tried to help her all I could to make it easier for her to work and keep house.

> I could not believe my ears when she told me that she had found someone else. The details are not important, but what she essentially said was that Hank had shown her for the first time what real sexual satisfaction was all about. He really turned her

on, made her feel like a different woman. According to her, I made love like a computer, thought only of myself.

She was a different woman, all right. It seemed to me that this could not be the woman I had trusted, had known to be so virtuous. What did it do to me? Can you imagine what I thought of myself? For the first six months I felt, for the first time in my life, that I was mortal—I died over and over again, and I wanted to hide my inadequacy as a man. I didn't want to go to work; I didn't want to see any of our friends. I was sure that I would never again want to have a close relationship with a woman.

Paul had been wounded, although the wound was not fatal. In response to it, after nearly a year, he struck out to bolster his self-image. "I guess I just got mad enough to want to prove I was OK," he said. He decided to "show her" through a succession of "one-night stands," hopping from one bed to another, with little or no regard for the lives and needs of these passing partners. This experience made Paul's journey longer, but he came to the place where he no longer felt he had to prove something in his relationships with women. Fully recovered, Paul now feels he is ready to trust a woman again and to seek a relationship that is not exploitive.

The problem of self-image is often more deep-rooted than it was with Paul. As one woman put it, "He told me I was stupid so often that I began to believe it." Whatever measure of strength or weakness a person has, the beginning point is knowing what you have to work with as you begin the processes of readjustment.

The age-old way of getting at a sagging self-image is to get a pencil and paper and begin listing the pluses and minuses like this:

Plus	Minus
A lot of people ask me for advice; so they must think I am intelligent.	I can't stand being put down—it makes me nervous.
Before marriage, I lived on next to nothing and I got by.	I've never had a really good-paying job.
I'm a reasonably attractive person when I work at it.	I don't like taking care of sick people.
My kids trust me.	I procrastinate a lot, do things at the last minute.
I'm a good driver; I've never had a serious accident.	I don't feel good when there's no one praising me.

Make your own list; make it honestly; but be fair to yourself. List everything you think of that has ever made you feel good, given you confidence, or brought you pleasure. List the major things that have disappointed you—in yourself or which made you feel you needed help. Deal with health matters, management matters, working matters, personal relationships, disposition, the way others see you, practical skills, interests.

Concentrate on that plus list. Think about the vitality that has seen you through some tough times, and try to assess what it was that got you through. Think about the determination that has kept you from faltering when things got tight. Think of the times when you have been recognized for having done something well; think of the people who have appreciated what you have done for them; consider the skills you have developed, the insights you have gained from your experiences.

You are on the road to getting acquainted with your personal resources. You may need some help in evaluating what these mean. Maybe you have played yourself down too much because of the way you feel right now. If so, find someone who has known you for a long time and ask that person to help you think it through—your parents or a brother or sister who will be fair and yet tough enough to be honest.

Then comes the step of applying what you have learned about yourself to your present situation. What personal resources do I have that can be useful in the managing side of my responsibilities? How much help do I need? What kinds of help? How much imagination do I have to help in thinking through how to get beyond the dead-end street where I find myself? What are the areas that I can improve? 19

Recently, in a group discussion about setting personal goals, one woman said,

> There's a woman on my street I admire so much. She always looks so neat, even when she's working in the yard. And she's such a *lady.* When she calls her kids, it is so gentle. Somehow I always manage to sound so coarse when I do it, and usually my hair is in curlers. I look up the street and see her, and I want to go hide.

It might be well to think about what attributes you admire in others. Are there some things about your own appearance and behavior you could work on? Try to be realistic here—you're not trying to be someone else. Rather, your goal should be to *be you,* but to strive for the best of you, not the mediocre or worst "you."

You've come a long way in your life. Regardless of whether you depended entirely on someone else for most of life's decisions or you did that only in certain areas of your life, you have gained insights and experiences that can now be called upon. There is no harm at all in admitting the need for help, but it is imperative to take stock first of what personal resources you have for coping with the readjustments in your life. Your reasoning power, your ability to relate to other people, your patience, your idealism, your practicality, your imagination, your physical strength, your sense of humor, your ability to care for other people—all these may be among your greatest resources as you turn to the business of getting your life on the move.

If, on the other hand, you are drawn irresistibly to the list of negatives that seem to overpower the positives, then look at them candidly and begin to think through ways to remove the negatives, improve your skills, and increase your positive resources.

For some, this process may lead to the development of skills and talents to become financially self-supporting. Others may reactivate hobbies and interests to provide outlets for making their lives more interesting. One woman decided to combine her hobby with earning additional income. She became an expert at tin-craft and began to design beautiful and useful gift items. She converted her garage into a craft shop and within a short time was consigning pieces of her work to local department stores. She is now lecturing at libraries and clubs about her craft and is receiving substantial fees for these appearances.

A man decided to turn his spare time into improving his chances for advancement. He enrolled in an evening school to learn computer programming. As a result, he is now employed in a much more interesting and challenging position.

It takes time to develop personal resources and to apply them. The most important ingredient of all in improving your self-image is within you—your determination to get out of the rut you may be in and to come alive to the world of possibilities that are yours for the taking.

Familial resources

Those closest to us, particularly parents if they are living, are the best resources we have to provide support during difficult times. That support can be in many forms: simply to be available to hear our problems and to offer help in solving them; to assist with the care of children occasionally; in some cases, to have a brother or sister accompany you to a court hearing or to other places where an emotional strain is expected.

Some people tell us they don't want to worry their parents with their problems. Others say their parents are too old or are too unstable in their health to be able to handle the problems. You do not

20

need to face your sense of injustice, your grief, or even your feelings of guilt without having human support from the primary members of your family. Sometimes the root of one's uneasiness in calling on parents for support stems from a long-held feeling that the parents in some way withheld affection during one's childhood years. There may be a dozen levels of feeling that block access to parents. But it is legitimate to call on them, for the parent-child relationship is the only relationship that cannot be broken. When you call on your parents in your time of need, you allow them to continue to fulfill their parenting role. If you have not been close to your family during your marriage, or if a serious break has occurred in your relationship, this may be a time to try to rework the relationship. You can "go home again." They may need to hear you say that you are ready to know what their side of your differences is; and then you can face them with your own feelings, your "side," in a genuine effort to rework your relationship to each other.

Even when members of your family live some distance from you, they can be available by letter or telephone (if visiting is not possible) to share your pain and to support you during a difficult time. That you trust them enough to share your need with them will bring them great joy in being needed. They still represent the best and most reliable resource you have.

Your children also have to be considered as a source of strength. They need to know you hurt sometimes—it makes it easier for them to admit they are hurting and to call on you to help them. If you were the one to initiate the divorce or separation, it also lets them know that doing so was painful for you—that it was something you felt had to be done and that you are paying a price for it.

Friends

A young woman said, "Don't tell me to call on my friends. I have only a very few who have stuck by me, and I think I've worn them out." During divorce, many couples who were friendly with a husband and wife who are splitting up find themselves in a terrible bind. They like both husband and wife. They want to be helpful but are afraid it will be viewed as taking sides. So they end up helping neither one. Or they don't offer, thinking that if they are asked, they will respond; and then it won't be as if they had initiated the contact. Try to explain to your friends that you are not expecting them to stop liking your spouse just because the two of you cannot live together, but that you need their help in a specific way; then ask if they are willing to stand by. It isn't necessary to scapegoat your former spouse; simply state your need. They can do no worse than refuse.

21

As for the good friends you may have worn out—yes, that is possible; you may have worn them out. But just as in marriage or any relationship, there has to be a giving and a getting for the relationship to be satisfactory over a long period of time. You will need to find some ways in which you *can* give something back—a fresh loaf of bread, a bouquet from your garden, a special thank-you note for even a trivial favor, always letting those friends know that you are aware of their importance to you. The loan of tools, help in a backyard project, and running an errand are all ways that you can assure them that you are anxious to find ways to balance the ledger, giving something back to them for the things they do for you.

Sometimes friends can become tired of hearing the same stories over and over again, no matter how much they care for you. Try not to overwork this telling, doing so only when you simply can't hold it in.

Then discuss only your own feelings and your perplexity. Other persons who are going through the same kind of thing you are are usually much more tolerant than others. We know several people who have made an alliance with a friend, agreeing to listen at any hour of the day or night when one or the other feels the need simply to talk to someone. Or they agree to call each other early in the morning just to talk about what the day holds for each of them and about ways in which they can be supportive.

22
A support group of persons who know about the pain of a broken relationship is, no doubt, the best place for this kind of discussion. There are many such groups around; but if there is not one in your community, you may wish to start one. We heard of one woman who is supporting her family by having "coffee and conversation" groups in her home twice a week. She charges $1.50 and prepares some simple sweets to serve with the coffee; and divorced, separated, or widowed people flock to her home, enjoying a place to talk with others who will be understanding. She started by inviting a few friends, and the idea caught on until she now has forty to fifty people each time. Not only is she helping solve her financial problem, but she is also making a lot of new friends.

Community resources

There are many sources of help in every community, even in some very small ones. Usually there are mental health clinics. Counseling services, both public and private, are available to you and for fees you are able to pay. Some clergy also do private counseling at no cost. If you are not sure which ones are available for this kind of help, call your local religious council and ask them to direct you.

Your physician is another source of information about support services, and the guidance and counseling staff in schools are always aware of such groups.

Financial resources

Many single parents are confronted immediately by radical changes in both their expenditures and their income. Often a person who has no experience in managing the family budget is now totally responsible. Added to this may be the problems of property settlement, insurance coverage, etc. Listed below are some helpful hints that you may wish to consider:

1. Get professional help to learn what your legal rights and responsibilities are, to assess your financial position, to work out steps you must take immediately, and to determine what long-term steps are needed. This may include finding someone to advise you about keeping or liquidating property. Ask your priest, minister, or rabbi to help you identify reliable professionals if you are unsure of where to turn.[1]

2. Based on the information you get from the assessment, make up a budget that is realistic and stay within it. If you've never made a budget, ask for help from family members or someone you trust.

23

3. Some companies are now allowing their employees to continue medical coverage for the family after separation or even divorce. Sometimes this may also include coverage for the former spouse until he/she remarries.

4. Except in an emergency, take your time in making decisions about money matters. Get more than one opinion, and be sure to consider all alternatives.

5. Women may want to check with one of the women's groups to see what help such groups have available for single women, which may include valuable assistance with financial matters.

6. Don't be too hasty in deciding to let "him/her" take everything in property settlements. The temptation is to give up in order to get the hassle over with, but you may later regret not holding out for some things, particularly some of

[1] See Appendix A for a sample listing of agencies that are available to provide information.

the household furnishings. Fairness on both sides will pay in the long run.

7. Don't let feelings of guilt cause you to "overgive" to a partner you have wounded. You can't buy forgiveness, and both of you have a life to continue.

8. Above all, be wary of people who come to *offer* professional help with your problems. There are many charlatans who feed on the pain of others. They watch newspaper accounts of death and divorces in order to sell questionable products or services. Seek your own help through reliable sources. Some of these salespersons may have legitimate businesses and may be useful resources; but if they come to you, check them out through the Better Business Bureau in your area. DON'T SIGN ANY AGREEMENT BEFORE YOU KNOW WHAT YOU ARE SIGNING. ASK TO KEEP THE AGREEMENT UNTIL YOU CAN HAVE YOUR LAWYER CHECK IT. If the salesperson is legitimate, he or she won't mind.

9. If you are in dire financial straits or have a financial emergency that is temporary, don't hesitate to call the local or county office of public assistance. There is absolutely no reason for you or your children to be hungry, and you can get help. You may also get information about day-care centers and, in some states, job retraining assistance.

10. If you can't afford a lawyer, call the local office of your bar association, and ask where you can go to get legal assistance. Tell the office your financial status, and the office will be helpful to you.

Spiritual resources

Many people tell us that they have drifted out of their church or synagogue because that organization is a couples' world and there is nothing to which they can relate. Others say that they dropped out because their clergyman, after the actual breakup of the marriage, had made them feel that they had let him down or had failed to utilize his counsel. They felt supported in the counseling before the breakup, but they were made to feel guilty or out of place afterward. They feel somehow that they are regarded as "sinners" by others, and they cannot bring themselves to go back to their congregation.

If your faith has ever been important to you, this is the time when you need it most. It can be a tremendous source of healing for you, and we would urge you to find a way back. Perhaps calling on your clergyman to help start a group for single parents would be a way to open the door. Most churches and synagogues are eager to find some way to bring in this large group of people, but they simply do not know how to do it. (The leader's guide, published as a companion to this book, may be helpful in that process.)

Many single parents feel that they have been abandoned even by God. But their relationship with God cannot be broken unilaterally. It takes two to form a relationship, and it takes both sides to break it. So long as you reach for them, the power of God and God's relationship to you are there for the claiming.

The most positive step you can take in starting to get your life moving again is to know that you are *not* alone in what you are trying to do. There are resources within yourself and around you that you have a right and a responsibility to utilize. It's up to you to identify those resources that can help you best and then to make the claim on them.

In his compelling book *White Banners,* Lloyd Douglas wrote:

> "Good use of a disappointment?" Paul [asked]. "I can't see what use you could make of a disappointment. If you can, I'd be glad to hear about it. I've had a plenty."
>
> "Well—a disappointment," ventured Hannah, feeling her way, cautiously, conscious of his half-derisive grin—"sometimes a disappointment closes a door in a person's face, and then he looks about for some other door, and opens it, and gets something better than he had been hunting for the first time."[2]

25

[2] Lloyd Douglas, *White Banners* (New York: P. F. Collier & Son Corporation, 1936), p. 73.

closing
the door

The elevator doors stand open. A slender woman, neatly but not too elegantly attired, stands within. She seems to be listening, then steps forward to look up and down the corridor. *Is someone coming? Maybe I should wait just a minute more.* She glances at the panel of call buttons, hears but ignores the insistent buzzing caused by those on floors below who await the coming of the elevator car. Still she waits, holding the button which prevents the doors from closing. One more quick check of the corridor and, finding no one there, she turns and reluctantly releases the "hold" button. The doors close, and quickly the car glides downward. It stops on several of the floors; people crowd in, pushing her to the back. Reaching the ground floor, the occupants move out, and she finds herself surrounded by people hurrying, busy, preoccupied with their own thoughts.

Moving to the revolving door, almost without willing it, she steps within the triangle of glass; and with a push provided by another triangle's occupant, she is propelled outside, beneath the building's canopy. With a sweeping bow the uniformed doorman grins broadly and greets her. "Welcome to the world," he said, "it's a great day to be alive!"

"Why, so it is," she replies, laughing. "I almost wish I had tried it sooner."

The woman on the elevator may be you—whether you are male or female. Are you reluctant to close the doors on a past relationship? Is it simply too painful for you to let go? We hope in this chapter to help you make the decision to close those doors and then to step out into the sunlight of a new life. This assumes, of course, that

> your former spouse is dead
>
> or
>
> there is no realistic hope or desire
> on either side for reconstituting a
> marriage.

We certainly would not urge you to close any doors as long as you are uncertain about your own or your former spouse's desire to go through with a divorce. If you have been separated for a long time and there is no other reason for delaying the divorce (such as religious beliefs, or because there is a financial advantage to one or both during separation as opposed to divorce, or that you cannot afford the legal fees), then we might ask you why not make the decision? If it has been some time since you talked about the situation, why not seek family counseling and call upon your former spouse to join you at the appointment?

Sometimes after the death of a spouse, the surviving partner finds it very difficult even to think about going on, about getting out of comfortable, secure patterns of living; the spouse may even at times be living in a world of make-believe, a world where things never change.

For many people this reluctance to give up the past (though, of course, we can never truly relinquish a past relationship) can become the invisible strands which hold one entrapped in a web of such emotional stress that it becomes more and more difficult to extricate oneself. Yet escape from that enmeshment is necessary if one is ever to move on, to live again in the present with all its possibilities.

R. D. Laing has put this well.[1] We have lived in a "family phantasy system" which has been meaningful to us, which has been tenable. Gradually, we have defined ourselves in terms of the relationship to the other. And even if we know that we have cut off something of what we could have been, we choose to see ourselves in this relationship. Thus the web, both good and ill, is spun around us and holds us in. But, says Laing, when events take place in which we no longer are supported in reality in this system that we have worked out for ourselves, we gradually come to the place where it is both impossible to stay and impossible to get out.

Even after the actual relationships have punctured the feelings

[1] R. D. Laing, *Self and Others* (New York: Barnes & Noble Books, 1961), chapter 2, "Phantasy and Communication."

and understandings of who we were in that former family system, we are yet held by invisible cords that seem so necessary for our well-being—and yet cords that trail listlessly in the current of life, lead to nothing stable, and hence, give no anchorage to check our drift. Still we hesitate to cut the cords loose.

The invisible cords must be identified and severed. And the truth is that this is the most difficult step anyone has to take in moving toward new goals and new opportunities. To return to our opening vignette, it is difficult to close the door on the past. It almost always calls for genuine courage, clearheaded realism, and personal strength. Betty told us,

> The first night was the hardest. I lay awake looking at the ceiling for hours thinking over what I had done. However, with each passing day I became more secure in my decision.

> I had left an era behind and was looking forward to the future with great optimism.

The first invisible cord for the separated parent has to be found in the ambivalence of love and hate toward the absent spouse. We often hear someone, like Anne, saying,

> The trouble is, I have a love-hate problem with my "ex." I hate him for what he has done to me; and yet I am still in love with him. I know that if he touched me, I would crumble. When he comes to pick up the kids, I put them on the porch and lock the door until after they are gone. That way I don't have to see him.

29

> At the same time, I know he is never coming back. He is living with another woman, and she is expecting his child. I can't concentrate on anything else. I spend hours thinking up ways that I might be able to get him to come back. Our house is like a tomb—it's no wonder the kids look forward to visiting with him. They have a great time, and then they come back here and hear me moaning. I'm filled with guilt, and I keep beating myself over the head thinking that maybe I could have done this or that differently and he wouldn't have left. I feel guilty about what kind of life I'm giving the kids. When they go to his apartment on the weekends, I am so lonely I could die.

It's no wonder Anne feels guilty and lonely. She has good reason to: she can't bring herself to let loose a past that is no longer there for her to grasp. She is spending so much time wishing, unrealistically, that she could undo what has been done—that she could reconstitute a marriage that is dead—that she has become a real burden to herself and to her children. Harry Truman once said, "People who spend all their time second-guessing themselves shouldn't get up in the morning." Well, Anne was getting up in the morning and was laying burdens on her children that were so heavy that they couldn't bear them. Because she refused to turn from the past, because she had almost grown used to feeding on her own self-pity, she was unconsciously giving unspoken signals to her children. While expecting their devotion to her because she was on the scene attending to their needs, in her self-pity she was giving signals that would make them feel disloyal to her whenever they looked forward to seeing their father.

It shocked Anne when her son one day decided that he would not go with his father for the weekend visits. His refusal gave Anne such deep anxiety that she decided to get some help. Gradually, she came to see that during all those months she had been coddling herself, trying to protect herself, by living in a fantasy world she had made for herself in which she could at times half-believe that this wasn't really happening to her, that he might come back to her. She began to see that she had to face the fact that she would be making her life for herself apart from her former husband. She was beginning to cut the strands so that the door could close on that marriage.

In a sense, Jack was doing the same thing when, in grief for his deceased wife, he gave up on life itself. He was healthy, handsome, and in his early fifties, with sufficient financial resources so that he wouldn't have to worry; but he decided that he had nothing more to do than to prepare to die. He put it like this:

> You see, my wife was a wonderful woman. She gave me everything I ever wanted in a wife. My mother died when I was very young, and I never knew what it could be like to have such companionship between a man and a woman. My father remarried, and he and my stepmother were always fighting; so they really lived separate lives. My wife and I did everything together. We didn't have a lot of social life because we were happy just to be together.
>
> Sometimes she would say that we ought to have so-and-so over for dinner, but usually I would suggest that it would be too much work, and we'd go out to dinner alone.
>
> I'd known she had something wrong for a long time, but she wouldn't go to the doctor. When she did, it was too late. I had trouble accepting her death—still keep thinking she's going to walk in the door. It's been two years, two lonely years. Still, I know I'll never find another woman like her.

30

Jack was experiencing the kind of pathological loneliness that so frequently plagues those who choose to live in the reality of their fantasy world instead of the world of what is actually happening. In his fantasy she *was* and she *was not* gone; he *could* and he *could not* expect her to enter again into his world. A mood of resignation springs up from this kind of ambiguous "wondering, doubting, trembling, fearing," which can only lead to a deeper sense of hopeless loneliness. Jack would rather wallow in that remorse than to close the door and turn toward life.

What would it mean to turn? It would mean accepting the reality of what has occurred. This need not mean any act of disloyalty to his former wife nor any detraction from the memory of a wonderfully satisfying relationship that may have been theirs. It does mean accepting death as a part of life and then moving toward what doubtless would constitute the third of his life span which lay before him.

All broken relationships require a period of grief, whether they are due to death, separation, or divorce. But grief has its day, and that day must yield to the sands of time and become part of the past as one turns toward a new day. Grief runs its course and comes to an end. Grief that is bottled up and left unspoken and unresolved, stored up to feed self-pity, will turn into what Shakespeare called "a plague of sighing and grief" that bids to break the heart.

Jack was no exception. His refusal to leave the fantasy world in which he chose to see himself as forever spent and emptied by grief, within which he cast himself in the role of suffering loneliness, could only lead to the logic of his own preparation for death. Yet, he had as much as a third of his life ahead of him, according to actuarial tables, and death does not always come when a person wills it. He could have a long time to be needlessly lonely. It isn't necessary for him to do so, and it brings no honor to the memory of the one who died. Jack's future lies in drawing back from the fantasy of himself as eternally mournful and turning toward the reality of what has happened, accepting both the fact of their happy life together and the fact of their separation by death. In that acceptance there can be the full honor to her whom he loved, with nothing detracted, and at the same time a cutting of the cords that bind him to the past in order to turn toward the future.

Grief Is a Part of Healing

A middle-aged woman called recently to say that she had asked her husband to leave, and she was greatly relieved when he was finally out of the house. "But," she added, "will you please tell my why I am so grief-stricken?" They had been married for thirty years and had produced five wonderful children. Both of them were in helping professions and were very well-educated, competent professionals. "I simply decided I could no longer mother my husband," she said. "I'm through with mothering after all those children."

The more she talked, the more this woman was able to answer her own question. She was grieving for the death of a relationship in which both of them had invested so much. When she was alone, she said, she cried for weeks until at last she decided that the tears had to end.

That does not mean, however, that the grieving process had necessarily ended. It will return, sometimes at the most unexpected times. There will be good days and bad days. Most people tell us that they know they are recovering when there are more good days than bad and when the bad days are not as devastating as they once were.

The shock was so great that I found it impossible to believe it, as it was completely unexpected. It took about six weeks before I was able to realize what had happened. After that, grief and pain would come and go. I had periods when I was surprised at how free from grief I felt. At other times the pain and heartache were very intense. I had been advised by a minister to be sure to cry. Prior to my husband's death, I shed tears only occasionally. I was amazed at the quantity of tears I shed after his death (especially when I was alone). I tried hard not to cry in front of people, although I did cry in front of my children. I felt it important that they know I loved and missed their father and sometimes they would cry with me. Now, a year and a half later, the pain is almost completely healed. Occasionally I will have a couple of bad days of tears and depression. I kept a record of this so that I could remind myself that it was only temporary and I would feel very different in a day or two. *Grief very definitely seems to come in cycles.*

In a hospital room a young woman, obviously well along in pregnancy, sat sobbing. Relatives crowded around her, trying hard to comfort her, to help her to accept her young husband's death. "It will be all right; we'll take care of you," said one.

"Don't cry; you're going to make yourself sick, and you have to think about the baby," said another.

The young woman tried to stop her crying, and the nurse on duty observed her anguish. Finally, the nurse asked all of the well-meaning relatives to leave her alone with the sobbing woman. She softly but firmly closed the door, turned to the young woman, and said,

"You have suffered a terrible loss. Cry—let it out—or you will never recover." The floodgates opened, and the woman cried until there were no tears. Months later, she returned to show the nurse her child.

"You saved me that day," she said, "I thought if I didn't cry, I would burst; and you were the only one who really understood."

Cry. Cry when you need to; release all of the tension that will build up from time to time. If you find that the crying goes on past a reasonable time (and that's hard to put a date on), or if it gets harder and harder to stop crying, you may need to find some help. The grieving needs to end some time, but it cannot be cut short.

> Brown: "Blessed are they that weep, for they shall laugh!" Only he that has wept can laugh! The laughter of Heaven sows earth with a rain of tears, and out of Earth's transfigured birth-pain the laughter of Man returns to bless and play again in innumerable dancing gales of flame upon the knees of God![2]

Unresolved Guilt

The cancerous spread of unresolved guilt can have the same effect. There is no question that guilt has its rightful place in the emotional balances of conscience. But it is there for a purpose: to redirect actions and relationships, to rebalance ledgers that have been weighted to a dangerous angle. But there are those who hang on to guilt as if it had become a permanent melancholic element in the personality. When guilt is centered in events that happened long ago and in connection with people who are no longer present to work it out, when there seems to be no apparent way to find release through rectifying the situation and asking forgiveness, the individual may give up and allow guilt to do permanent damage.

33

Guilt, like grief, may often be a clinging to the past and an unwillingness to close the doors to the past. The only real emotion that is left after the numbness of betrayal or abandonment may be the emotion of guilt. To remove it would be to close the door on the past.

What makes one feel guilty? When this is asked of groups of single parents, one answer always comes:

> I feel guilty because my kids are growing up with only one parent; and I think they need two.

Implied in that kind of statement is the implicit acceptance of guilt that the partner abandoned the family, that the partner died, or that the partner became alcoholic, abusive, etc. It is saying with one

[2] Eugene O'Neill, *The Great God Brown,* from *Nine Plays* (New York: The Modern Library, imprint of Random House, Inc., 1941), p. 374.

side of the mind, *What has happened to me is unfair. I have been wronged;* and with the other saying, *In some way it was my fault. Had I conducted myself differently, it wouldn't have happened; and now the children are hurt, deprived by the consequences.*

This kind of guilt cannot be sustained unless one has built a concept of what has happened which is part factual and part imaginative, in which one places himself or herself into roles of remorseful suffering and feeding upon self-pity.

Some guilt has a valid basis: it is conscience extracting its price. Deserved guilt must lead to some form of balancing of the scales. There is no way that a person can stop history, back it up, and do it over again after having learned the nature of the mistake from living through the consequences. That is not a possibility, however successful the person is in holding a fantasy framework in the mind, in constantly reliving the scenes and continuously trying out the various alternatives to see if some other would have been better. The resolution of this kind of enervative thinking, with all of its pain and all of the induced loneliness, requires the courage to accept what has happened, take appropriate steps to balance the scales, and begin to close the door.

You cannot assuage your guilt by rationalizing that it is better for the children to have only one parent in the house than to have two who are constantly at odds with each other. Nevertheless, adequate parenting can be provided by one reliable parent who is not filling the children's lives with anger and bitterness, self-pity and self-rejection. There is no way that unresolved guilt can be hidden; try as you will, it will come out. As Shakespeare said in Hamlet,

> So full of artless jealousy is guilt,
> It spills itself in fearing to be spilt.

Maturity comes with an admission of guilt—acceptance of the acts of the past as the best that could be done at that time—by taking steps to right any wrong and then turning toward the future sobered, wiser, and looking to the future with hope. You are never going to be both father and mother to your children, but it is possible to parent with integrity. And if the other parent is still living, it is possible, as we will see in a later chapter, to hold that parent accountable for continuing availability to the children.

To the person who says,

> I feel guilty because I left my husband (or wife). Maybe I should have tried harder to make the marriage work,

we have to say that maybe you should have; and if so, you may want to rethink your decision. But if the marriage is now dead, if you aren't considering going back, or if your spouse has taken the steps that make it impossible to go back, then there is nothing to be gained by walking around with a load of guilt on your back for the rest of your life. You have to say with confidence, "I did the best I could with the resources I had available." We hear so many parents saying that the greatest fear they have in raising their children is that they will make a wrong decision. Every parent does, and some of us are honest enough to admit it. But if we did the best we could at the time, that's all we can be expected to do.

I feel guilty because I believe that marriage is for life, and here I am involved in a divorce; and I'm already thinking that I might marry again someday. How can I face the church?

This is a very difficult issue. When this statement was made in a single parent group, a very wise counselor—herself divorced—advised:

You have got to decide what your ground is and where your values are. If you are feeling that it would be wrong for you to remarry, you have only two choices—you will either have to rethink your values or be prepared to stand your ground.

Nobody can do it for you. You have to face this by yourself, and you had better do it soon.

35

Guilt can be destructive if it is not dealt with honestly and openly. Are there some steps you can take that will help to relieve the pain you have caused someone else? Is your former mate deliberately loading you with guilt beyond reasonable cause? Guilt can be a constructive emotion if it causes one to take some steps for helping to heal the wounds one has inflicted on another or if it forces one to grow to the point of taking a different course the next time.

I feel guilty because I didn't believe my husband when he said he thought something was wrong with him. I should have insisted that he see a doctor sooner. I almost feel responsible for his death.

This is the most fruitless kind of self-punishment. Your hindsight is better than your foresight. Your husband was an adult, and you were not his keeper. If he knew he was ill and didn't do anything about it, probably your prodding would have been to no avail.

Standing at the door, unable to separate the emotional ties to the past from legitimate memory of the past, unable to free oneself to push the button to move to another level, to break from the familiar floor of self-understanding, you may experience that acute form of

loneliness that rises up in the middle of the night at the sound of a voice, a familiar scene, or even a fragrance you remember.

Handling Loneliness

Loneliness can be dealt with if you are serious about cutting the ties to the past and trying to prepare for the future. Everyone is lonely at one time or another; but the question is, What do you do about it?

Let's begin with the obvious. There is a difference between being alone and being lonely. All of us need periods of being alone, to be able to sort out our thoughts and decide on what ground we are able to stand. Only the person who knows how to stand alone is suitable for shared companionship. There are times when being alone sounds like the most delicious of conditions. The difference is that being alone usually is a matter of choice, while being lonely usually implies a more negative, imposed condition.

Loneliness is real. At times it is just uncomfortable; at times it stifles; at times it renders one dysfunctional. It comes at unexpected times, with swiftness, triggered by a sound, a familiar object, an event, reaching out a hand to find no one else beside you in bed, the sound of the alarm in the morning, or the very stillness of the early morning hours. It is real; it is painful. And simply wishing it away will not make it happen.

Loneliness is of the nature of a psychological pain. It is a feeling of lostness and helplessness. It has rootage in the soil of rejection and despair. A child, leafing through a magazine and trying to describe the feelings of persons in the pictures, comes to a haunting face of a child in a war-torn country and says, "He is lonely; he is wishing." And the child's wisdom cuts through all our attempts to describe how the lonely person feels. How true—that the person who feels lonely is wishing for something! That is the beginning point of helping loneliness to go away.

When you feel lonely, what are you wishing for?

We asked a group of newly single persons to identify the times when they felt most lonely. This is a sample of what they listed:

When the car won't start (I'm wishing someone
   dependable were there to make it start)

When the budget won't balance, the bills come
   in, and I feel panic coming on (I'm wishing
   for someone to share the financial load)

In the morning when I wake up and know it's going
   to be the same kind of day as yesterday
   (I'm wishing for some relief from boredom)

In the middle of the night when I reach out and
   realize I'm alone in the room (I'm longing for
   intimacy)

When I see a couple dancing or even walking
   along hand in hand (I'm wishing for the joy
   of belonging)

Holidays—any holiday (I'm remembering happy
   times and wishing I could recapture them)

37

Writing things down, incidentally, is the best way to try to analyze the problem. Make a list of your own, remembering when it is that you feel most lonely and then adding to the list the times that such feelings are most difficult. Don't hurry this process. You are not going to be able to overcome these feelings overnight. But when you have a list that seems to represent your usual pattern, you may want to try to group these feelings into three or four categories. These might be:

I feel lonely when:
   —being alone triggers the fear of personal failure.
   —guilt that hasn't been dealt with is stimulated.
   —demands expose distrust of self and even self-hatred.
   —inner conflicts and tensions are aroused.
   —when memories of happier times come flooding back.

When you have gotten this far with your analysis, you are ready to begin working on some solutions to the problem. Trying to solve it all at once won't work; it will only make it more confusing. So start with something you can do tomorrow, letting the days that follow take their turn. Let's suppose, for example, that being alone at night is hard for you. You miss the intimacy; you need to talk with someone after the kids are in bed; everything in the bedroom reminds you of times when you and your spouse were together; and sometimes you are afraid. What can you do? One group of single parents made this list of suggestions out of their own experiences:

1. Be careful of overeating and stimulants that tend to make sleep difficult.

2. Think ahead. Decide in advance what you will do if you wake up in the middle of the night and are feeling lonely. Plan for an alternative to lying sleepless in bed—something to read, a letter to write, some handwork to finish, something that will require attention. Have the materials handy. Better to spend an hour in this fashion than to toss in the emotional doldrums of loneliness.

3. Rearrange the room in a fashion quite different from what it was when your spouse was there. Select color schemes, a picture, books, light stand, etc., to your own distinctive taste.

4. Be sure the bed and bedding are comfortable and pleasant. Pamper yourself a little with a long bath and a splash of after-bath lotion.

5. If you are apt to be afraid, have the locks on your windows and doors checked to see how easily they can be opened. Replace them if necessary. Have some hard-to-tamper-with lights installed outside that can be turned on with a switch near your bed. These are good safety measures in any family. You should also be sure you and the children have a plan for what you will do in case of fire. Local fire departments have excellent booklets about fire safety, and you and your children can visit the firehouse and then study them together.

6. If you have a friend who is going through the same adjustments you are, it might be well to talk over the possibility of being able to call each other at any hour when you simply *have* to have someone to talk to. Don't overdo this; agree that it will be only when there is no other alternative.

7. Arrange with neighbors or friends who live close by to be able to call them if you have illness in the middle of the night and need help. Everybody likes to be needed, and you will find them surprisingly open to this possibility.

WARNING: Don't fall into the trap that many people do when they are alone, lonely, feeling trapped—resorting to alcohol or some other drug to relieve the pain. Above all, recognize your vulnerability and ask for help when you need it.

None of these suggestions, of course, deals with the matter of your longing for intimacy, your need for sexual satisfaction. As indicated earlier, we will deal with this in more depth later in the book. For now, we have to say that there is no easy or quick solution to this need. You are still making the adjustment of becoming "uncoupled"; and until you have come to terms with that adjustment, you are not ready for another relationship. TAKE YOUR TIME. There is nothing that will bring you more anguish and compound your problems faster than running into someone else's arms and bed before you have dealt with who you are, what you want out of life, and what the ground of your life will be.

There are no magic formulas or rules that will make it easy for you or that can guarantee a successful outcome. Bed hopping is a poor substitute for intimacy and may indeed prevent intimacy. Also, both men and women may have many opportunities for sexual relationships. Don't be too surprised if the earliest offers come from your married friends. The coupled world is loaded with individuals whose own marriages are shaky, and they see you as someone who "needs" their help. No matter how attractive these married persons seem to you, avoid involvement with them like the plague—unless you want to spend a lot more nights crying.

Finally, the answer to how you overcome loneliness is with you. You need to be happy with yourself, to like yourself, to reestablish an image of yourself that will give you the confidence you need to seek out new friendships, both male and female. You may not be ready yet to look for a new set of friends; and if not, wait awhile. The time will come. You have already found, we're sure, that your old friends are not seeking you out as they once did. That's not because they think there is something wrong with you; but sometimes it's because they simply don't know what to do with you. We have all become accustomed to thinking that if we invite a single person, then we are somehow obligated to find a single of the opposite sex to be that person's "partner." A single, attractive woman may seem to be a threat to a wife who knows her husband has a roving eye; the same is true of a single man. The husband who is not sure of his own ground with his wife may hesitate to invite a single man into his home. For many others, it is a matter of not wishing to take sides.

The time will come when you will have to accept the fact that you are single and will have to seek out other singles for companionship. In many ways, your friends who fail to invite you to their homes may be doing you a favor. If they are too protective, you will never get the courage you need to start a new life for yourself. One woman, a widow of two years, told us:

> My friends were absolutely wonderful. They invited me to everything—to dinner, to the theater, to their family gatherings. And for a while that was great. It took a long time, but I finally realized that they were not really doing me a favor with their kindness. I could have stayed in that cocoon forever. I finally had to say to them, "I am so grateful to you for helping me to get through these terrible months. But the time has come for me to get out there in that singles' world. I want to see you once in a while, and I want always to be your friend; but I've got to make it on my own."

Most of her friends accepted her decision, and she feels they were really relieved. Others seemed hurt, but she kept in contact and, except for a very few, has a better relationship with them than ever.

This chapter has focused on the need for examining the emotions you are experiencing in the wake of a broken relationship and the possibilities for helping you deal with them. Before you can be ready for moving on, for looking at the possibilities before you in the future, we want to help you take a more candid look at yourself and your response in love, in an intimate relationship.

This kind of self-examination may be helpful to you in sorting out some of the "whys" of what has happened to you. You may be able to see what some of the dynamics were in your former relationship—why it was bad and perhaps doomed from the beginning or why it was good. That, in turn, will make possible a clearer understanding of what you may be seeking in future relationships.

you and your love

The need to love and be loved runs very deep in our human nature. Men and women are born with the capacity to give and to receive love and to know that they are doing it. That's why it hits so hard when our love relationship has ended or appears to be running down, growing tired or dying. Then it is that we are apt to ask the unanswerable questions: Why? Why me? Have I lost the capacity to love? Or was I *ever* really in love?

Little wonder that the poets outdo themselves with figures of speech to describe love! A composite of phrases over several centuries would read: love is a kiss, a mood, a proud and gentle thing, a sickness, a spirit compact of fire, is blind, is doomed to mourn, is the beginning, is heavy, is indestructible, is like a dizziness, is a red red rose, is like the measles, is strong as death, is sweet for a day, is coldest of critics, an enchanted dawn, the gift of God, the jewel that wins the world, the mellow glow of autumn, is many splendored.

Love is so many things to so many people and so many things to each of us at different times in our lives because it flows from the kind of person we are. The kind of person we are determines the kind of love we expect from another and the kind we are prepared to give. Since no two people are exactly alike, it is not surprising that the expectations of love are never exactly alike nor that the giving and receiving of love change as people change. One woman—let's call her Nell—summed it up like this:

He doesn't talk to me anymore; he doesn't take me seriously at all. Oh, he talks but he talks *at* me—about the weather, his job, politics, the car, sports, everything—but he doesn't talk *to* me. He used to. There was a time when he couldn't do enough; everything he did or said seemed to make me feel he was glad I was his wife. And I did the same with him. I'd show him things that would remind us of experiences we had had, and we shared our own understanding that only he and I knew. But no more. It's different now. At times I think he doesn't want me at all, or maybe I'm just beginning to see that he never did really want me or the warmth I had to give from the start. We can't talk about our feelings at all anymore.

It's so easy in the beginning to read into the relationship what we are hungry to receive; and it is easy to fall into the mistake of trying to give what the other one wants to receive even when we don't have it to give. It is not at all unusual for people far advanced in the years of marriage to discover that they have been asking things of their partner that he or she is incapable of giving.

One husband and wife moving toward an uncontested divorce proceeding began thinking through what had happened so that they could offer responsible parenting to the children. It turned out that he had been raised in a cool, "no-touch," reserved family. His father had died at an early age, and he could not remember how his parents related to each other. But her family had been red-blooded and volatile, full of laughter, squabbles, excitement, and action. For him mealtime had been a quiet, thoughtful time; for her it had been the most exciting time of the day when the whole family "shared" at once with teasing, confronting, testing. He longed for a quiet life with an intellectual companion who shared his tastes in the arts, politics, and world affairs; she wanted a warm, spontaneous enthusiast who would give verve to life, ecstatic pleasure in sex, and the stimulation she always enjoyed in the unexpected.

When this couple separated, each member carried a feeling of guilt. They didn't hate each other really, but they simply couldn't make it work. Neither had known what the other expected; had they known, they might have tried to meet each other's needs. At least now the better understanding made it easier for them to talk to their children about the cause of the break-up and to achieve a parenting responsibility that did not put the children in the middle.

Some things change in all of us over the years; and yet, there are basic patterns that persist and give us identity. The experience we had in being parented, the inheritance we have received from the past, and our cumulative experiences over the years give identity to our character and personality as we relate to others.

Expectations of Love

Psychology Today ran an interesting article in October, 1974, which described five ways in which people give and receive love.[1] These constructs of love were based on a study of couples who had come to a clinic. The types of love identified suggest patterns of personality which lie behind what we expect to give and receive in love. While these constructs should never be thought of as rigid molds or forms by which to judge ourselves, and no one ever fits into any one of the patterns exactly, they do help us gain a kind of "no-fault" perspective on what we expect to give and receive in love and how we have experienced it in the past.

1. *EROS—The Classical Lover*

Eros had a relatively happy childhood, felt little discontent with life at any time, and is emotionally secure. From the moment of meeting, Eros is strongly attracted to the loved one, feels the relationship was "meant to be." From that moment Eros thinks constantly about the beloved, wants to be near the beloved every day, wants to share feelings, make plans, and discuss everything of interest with the beloved. Very early Eros is sure that the relationship will be permanent and is ready to speak of the love and to make a commitment to an enduring relationship. Eros is not bothered by differences, doesn't feel anxiety about the relationship ended, and believes in the sincerity of the partner. Sexual intimacy comes early in the relationship, and Eros feels that the level of sexual rapport is a test of love, and yet is eager to work at ways of making sex more complete and satisfactory. For Eros, love is no part-time activity. The enjoyment is in touching, being near, experiencing the beloved.

Eros shows up in both male and female lovers. Always it is an abiding, intense love relationship in which the lover expects to give and to receive with the whole being. Because of this intense feeling, the Eros lover will not face conflict with the loved one but will attempt to smooth it over. The Eros lover is quite capable of terminating the relationship if it turns out that no love is returned.

2. *STORGE—A Cool Cat*

Storge doesn't go looking for a loved one but rather finds the beloved in the midst of normal, enjoyable activity. Natural companionship is the key to the love relationship. Storge had a happy childhood and is content with life. Storge was in no hurry to find a mate and didn't think about the relationship very much at first.

43

[1] John Alan Lee, "The Styles of Loving," *Psychology Today,* vol. 8, no. 5 (October, 1974), pp. 43-51.

Storge was willing to find a suitable partner but didn't have any real preconception of what the partner would be like. Storge was comfortable with the beloved from the beginning but never felt a compulsion to see the beloved daily nor to avoid the loved one. Storge isn't strong on discussing feelings, displaying emotion, or sharing future plans; and while sexual intimacy is enjoyable, it is not of the highest priority in the relationship.

Storge is faithful, dependable, gives constant devotion, but would not understand nor tolerate abuse from the beloved. Jealousy is not in Storge's make-up. There would be few differences or anxieties in a relationship with Storge because the rapport and attraction for each other are based on mutual understanding and compatibility. If the relationship should break up, there would be no lasting bitterness.

Storge is quite secure and would not flatter the loved one by showing dependency or by displaying emotional need. The steady, faithful presence might seem to border on taking love and the loved one for granted, but the mate can expect thoughtful attention from Storge, as well as care and consistent planning for activities of mutual interest.

3. PRAGMA—Appreciation of the Loved One

Pragma's love is a first love for which there had been a clear image in advance and a patience in finding the right one. There is a sense of security in the love and a confidence in the partner's interest. Pragma sensed from the beginning that the relationship would be permanent, but, as in the case of Storge, there is no need to see the loved one every day. Sex is not all-important to Pragma, although it is enjoyed and efforts to improve the techniques of bringing the partner to more satisfaction are in order. Love is not the highest priority, and Pragma would not "give all" for love.

Pragma does not reassure the mate constantly of the love; there is a sense of security in the giving and the receiving of love. Pragma doesn't go for touching and being touched and is somewhat bored by the idea of talking all the time about love.

This makes for a reliable companion who takes life as it comes and finds meaning and security in a love relationship with someone who enjoys the same kind of life. Pragma and Storge are much alike, except that Pragma made a deliberate search for the right kind of mate, while Storge discovered the love out of a natural, shared companionship.

4. MANIA—One Who Loves with a Passion

Mania needs to be loved deeply and emotionally. The childhood was unhappy; and Mania is a worrier, filled with anxiety and never sure that the loved one accepts or returns love. There is a capacity for self-rejection and a discontent with life generally.

Strong initiative is not taken in the beginning to develop the love relationship, and there is seldom a defined image in advance of the person to love. Once committed, however, there is preoccupation with the thoughts of love coupled with an uncertainty as to how it is received. There is a strong desire to see the loved one every day, every moment; and yet, there is a hesitancy to discuss or display the feelings about love, lest they not be accepted.

Mania needs—requires—the anchorage of shared love. The need is great enough so that all warnings of coming trouble in the relationship would likely be ignored. As for terminating the relationship, Mania would never take the initiative—there is too much dependency upon the security of love.

This one constantly presses the beloved for a greater show of feeling and commitment and shows signs of extreme jealousy. Mania is never a cool, indifferent person but rather an intensely emotional partner. Because of the insecurity, Mania would not likely risk sexual involvement early, although the declaration of love could be well ahead of the partner's. If the love is returned, then love would prove to be the most important matter in life, absolutely essential to well-being. Love with Mania might be exhausting and might seem to lack awareness of the beloved's needs; but one would never doubt that Mania loved his or her mate.

5. LUDUS—Enjoy, Enjoy!

Ludus is not looking for security, nor for a partner based on a preconceived notion of what the partner will be like. Ludus enjoys sex and enters a relationship for the sake of joy and satisfaction. The quality of the love is likely to be measured by the quality of the sex experience; and yet the enjoyment of the total person is as important as the sex act itself. The fun is also in the chase. Ludus doesn't like to get too serious about the relationship and doesn't need constant contact with the beloved. Ludus doesn't mind discussing feelings, but the partner would encounter some difficulty in talking about future plans or in having a depth discussion on any subject.

Ludus wouldn't urge the mate into a deep commitment but would enjoy a looser rein, a more casual approach. It follows that Ludus is not possessive and is not jealous, although the blame would fall on the partner rather quickly if there were difficulties in the relationship. Ludus would rather seek a new partner than work too hard on improving the techniques of the sex life. There would not be

45

much talk about love. Love is to be enjoyed, not to be talked about. In that sense love is not of the greatest interest.

If the relationship did break up, Ludus would not have lasting bitterness. Ludus would marry if a partner is found who shares the outlook on the love relationship, but the "open marriage" concept would be more attractive than the traditional patterns of constancy.

The Patterns of Love

There are many gradations that can be drawn among these five categories of love that are described above. With a little imagination a person can see that some of the combinations would get along together only if there was a consistent effort to make it work. For example, Mania and Ludus would have to agree to get their feelings, which they both are reluctant to discuss, out in the open on a regular basis if the relationship were to stand up.

Probably you have found some points of identification of yourself and your former partner in one or another of these generalized word pictures. Even though no person fits neatly into any one of these categories, most people can identify with one of the ways of loving more than the others. This does not mean that an individual is locked into some rigid framework or that one of these categories is "better" than another. It does mean that each of us should see that what we expect from the person we love and what we offer of ourselves are rooted in prevailing patterns of our lives. We can't just turn these things on and off at will. Who we really are is expressed in our love.

Few people have stopped to take a close look at what they really expected of their marriage partner before the marriage, and certainly there are few who have connected expectations of love with the human needs that condition those expectations. If you ask yourself what you really wanted from a past love relationship, you may discover that what you were asking and expecting was unfair, that the partner was incapable of giving what you asked, or that you yourself were not giving back enough to meet the partner's needs. The love relationship that is not based on reciprocal fairness soon becomes a distorted relationship. Each person in a relationship must feel that he or she is getting as well as giving, lest the sense of imbalance, of being cheated, in time cause the relationship to disintegrate. If you feel that one of the styles of love described above comes close to your own, then you should ask yourself, "Am I asking for something in love that I am unwilling to give?"

Looked at in this light, you may feel that you would like your love to have some of the characteristics of all five of the types

46

described. Most people show some tendencies like those in all five of these categories, although one or two usually stand out. It would be rare for one person to be characterized equally by all five of these composites, simply because the kind of love a person expresses and desires is rooted in that combination of endowment, experience, values, and actions that we call *Personality*. Persons who come on with intense, passionate love will be quite different in personality and background from those who offer a cool, thoughtful, detached form of love.

Childhood experiences help to shape these needs for love. Relationships with parents and primary associates are the places where the meaning and expression of love have been learned and where the degree of trust that can be given is understood. For example, it would be difficult for a person who has known the security of a caring relationship which left room for individual growth and independence to move to a style of love that is passionately possessive. Likewise, it would be just as difficult for a person whose family of origin was one where distrust and discord were the norm, or who had experienced abandonment, to give himself or herself freely to a relationship that involved trust and sharing and enjoyment of the other. In rare instances, this crossover can and does happen, but it takes a great deal of patience and self-understanding; it requires the cooperation of both parties and a determination to see it through.

47

For some people, an understanding of the way in which the forms of love are rooted in the fabric of life itself has provided new insight into why a former love relationship was unsuccessful. For others, particularly widowed persons, new insight may be gained in knowing why their relationship with the deceased was deeply satisfying.

> For three years I found a sad satisfaction in telling myself and my friends how dreadful my wife had been to go off with another man after awakening love in me—because, she said, I did not satisfy her. It made me feel better to put the blame on her. Now I am beginning to see our relationship was unlikely and doomed from the beginning.

> I did resent the fact that she seemed to want my attention almost twenty-four hours of the day. Many of the angry scenes we had centered in my angry demand that she stop smothering me. I thought she was covering up something by being so emotional all the time. I didn't know then that she really lived at a different emotional level that was as legitimate as mine.

In the beginning I was flattered by her insatiable desire for sex. It was only later that I realized that her appetite for sex was too much for me. I wanted her to change her nature for my sake. It didn't occur to me then that I had just as much reason to try to change myself.

Perhaps you will want to ask yourself the question again: What kind of person do I want for a love partner? Which of the groups of characteristics seems to come closest to what I want? Having answered that, then reflect on the reasons why you selected the one you did. Were you really reflecting what you wanted someone else to give to you, or were you including also what you were willing to give to the other person? Now you are ready to answer the important question: Which of the five types of persons do I most resemble in terms of what I am prepared to give in a love relationship?

Consideration of this kind of question sometimes causes a person to take a really hard look at himself or herself which can be very productive. If a love relationship has grown stale for you, or if a past love remains an undigested lump in the pit of your stomach, you may benefit from this kind of self-examination.

We're not suggesting here that you engage in some kind of do-it-yourself psychoanalysis, but rather that as part of your healing process, you may be able to rid yourself of some unnecessary guilt by a better understanding of what makes you or your former spouse tick. Understanding behavior doesn't necessarily mean you can excuse irresponsible action, but understanding it may allow you to put to rest once and for all some unwarranted self-doubt.

Who you are, what you are, what you need, and what you value are all part of what you do. The failure of one marriage doesn't have to make you conclude that you are incapable of making another relationship work. On the other hand, because your first marriage was good—unless you understand what made it good—does not necessarily mean that the next one will be.

The Simplistic Answers

Perhaps you are one who believes that it is possible to bypass all of this self-examination by simply assuring yourself, "I will not make that mistake again," or "I will put the memory away and not let it interfere in a new relationship." There are many ways to refer to this attitude; but whatever form it takes, there can be little hope for fulfillment in the future as long as the role you had in the past relationship is ignored. It's much easier to blame the other person than to look at your own part in the breaking of a relationship. You can't ignore or erase what has happened to you. You can learn from it and grow into a more interesting, more caring, and more lovable person.

You may have decided that it would be safer to look for a relationship with a person who is just the opposite of your former mate, the rationale being, "I don't intend to get myself mixed up the next time with another emotional female who will get fed up with me and take off one day with another guy." You tell yourself that this time you'll find a love who is a devoted homebody. "I don't care if she's ugly; at least she'll be mine." Deep down, however, you know that you like a woman attractive enough for other men to envy you. You will have to face the hard fact that there was something wrong in your marriage or else your wife would never have been attracted to that other man. That hurts. It's a low blow, you may think. Perhaps it is, but it's probably true. Next time you won't ignore the danger signals; next time you may be ready to find out where you are failing to meet her needs. Maybe you'll agree early in your relationship to talk about feelings; maybe you'll risk telling her your feelings.

Another of the simplistic approaches that some formerly married persons take is to decide not to reveal their true selves but to try to match their responses to what they perceive the other person is looking for.

I really wanted to get married again. I loved being married the first time. My husband was so good to me; he always seemed to know my needs before I knew myself. I waited for two years and then decided that it was time for me to make a new life for myself.

I could not face the possibility of marrying another man who would remind me of Joe. I decided that the thing to do was to find somebody totally different. When I met Don, he made it clear that he was looking for a wife and that he wanted a wife who lived her own life and would allow him space enough for his.

He was such an exciting kind of man. Every woman in our singles' group had made a play for him. I had heard from others that he was scared of clinging women. Well, I played it cool, and he liked my act.

We were married, and within three months it was over. I never could depend on him to be home when he promised. He simply couldn't take my "hassling" him, he said. He felt cheated, and I guess I can't blame him. The trouble is, I was sure I could make him over.

What possible chance does a love relationship have that is based

49

	Statement	Eros	Ludus	Storge	Mania	Ludic Eros	Storgic Eros	Storgic Ludus	Pragma
1	You consider your childhood less happy than the average of peers	R		AN	U				
2	You were discontent with life (work, etc.) at time your encounter began	R		AN	U	R			
3	You have never been in love before this relationship					U	R	AN	R
4	You want to be in love or have love as security	R	AN			AA	AN	AN	U
5	You have a clearly defined ideal image of your desired partner	AA	AN	AN	AN	U	AN	R	AA
6	You felt a strong gut attraction to your beloved on the first encounter	AA	R	AN	R		AN		
7	You are preoccupied with thoughts about the beloved	AA	AN	AN	AA		R		
8	You believe your partner's interest is at least as great as yours	U	R	AN			R	U	
9	You are eager to see your beloved almost every day; this was true from the beginning	AA	AN	R	AA		R	AN	R
10	You soon believed this could become a permanent relationship	AA	AN	R	AN	R	AA	AN	U
11	You see "warning signs" of trouble but ignore them	R	R		AA		AN	R	R
12	You deliberately restrain frequency of contact with partner	AN	AA	R	R	R	R	U	
13	You restrict discussion of your feelings with beloved	R	AA	U	U	R		U	U
14	You restrict display of your feelings with beloved	R	AA	R	U	R		U	U
15	You discuss future plans with beloved	AA	R	R				AN	AA
16	You discuss wide range of topics, experiences with partner	AA	R				U	R	AA
17	You try to control relationship, but feel you've lost control	AN	AN	AN	AA	AN	AN		

Consider each characteristic as it applies to a current relationship that you define as love, or to a previous one if that is more applicable. For each, note whether the trait is *almost always* true (AA), *usually* true (U), *rarely* true (R), or *almost never* true (AN).

To diagnose your style of love, look for patterns across characteristics. If you consider your childhood less happy than that of your friends, were discontent with life when you fell in love, and very much

50

	Eros	Ludus	Storge	Mania	Ludic Eros	Storgic Eros	Storgic Ludus	Pragma
18 You lose ability to be first to terminate relationship	AN	AN		AA	R	U	R	R
19 You try to force beloved to show more feeling, commitment	AN	AN		AA		AN	R	
20 You analyze the relationship, weigh it in your mind			AN	U		R	R	AA
21 You believe in the sincerity of your partner	AA			U	R	U		AA
22 You blame partner for difficulties of your relationship	R	U	R	U	R	AN		
23 You are jealous and possessive but not to the point of angry conflict	U	AN	R		R	AN		
24 You are jealous to the point of conflict, scenes, threats, etc.	AN	AN	AN	AA	R	AN	AN	AN
25 Tactile, sensual contact is very important to you	AA			AN	U	AN		R
26 Sexual intimacy was achieved early, rapidly in the relationship	AA			AN	AN	U	R	U
27 You take the quality of sexual rapport as a test of love	AA	U	AN		U	AN	U	R
28 You are willing to work out sex problems, improve technique	U	R		R	U		R	U
29 You have a continued high rate of sex, tactile contact throughout the relationship	U		R	R	U	R		R
30 You declare your love first, well ahead of partner	AN	R	AA	AA				
31 You consider love life your most important activity, even essential	AA	AN	R	AA		AA	R	R
32 You are prepared to "give all" for love once under way	U	AN	U	AA	R	AA	R	R
33 You are willing to suffer abuse, even ridicule from partner	AN	R	AA			R	AN	
34 Your relationship is marked by frequent differences of opinion, anxiety	R	AA	R	AA	R	R		R
35 The relationship ends with lasting bitterness, trauma for you	AN	R	R	AA	R	AN	R	R

51

want to be in love, you have "symptoms" that are rarely typical of eros and almost never true of storge, but which do suggest mania. Where a trait did not especially apply to a type of love, the space in that column is blank. Storge, for instance, is not the *presence* of many symptoms of love, but precisely their absence: it is cool, abiding affection rather than *Sturm und Drang*.

on fraud? How can trust build between two people when one of them is playing a role? And trust is a fundamental part of any close relationship. If I trust you, then I am able to risk letting you know the best of me and the worst of me. I am willing to share all that I have with you, because I feel certain that you will not take advantage of me.

Regaining the capacity to trust another is one of the most difficult of all adjustments that the single parent has to make, especially when a trusted spouse has let you down. This is not hard to understand, for having been burned once, it is only natural that you would avoid the fire. There's no such thing as instant trust—unfortunately you can't get it in a ready-mix form. Trust has to be developed slowly and nurtured and tested and tested again. But if you ever hope to love again, you are going to have to find the courage to take that risk.

For many people, one marriage is enough. Either they feel that the first one was so good that they don't want to push their luck a second time, or that the first one was so bad that they don't need that grief anymore.

We can't argue with that. Nor do we find fault with the person whose religious beliefs make remarriage out of the question. Your own values, your own needs will be your guiding principles. All we are asking is that you make the attempt to understand what you brought to your former marriage, what you gave to that relationship. Your self-image is closely tied to that understanding, and it can have a profound impact on the rest of your life.

Your style of loving and your manner of relating to a spouse have echoes of similarity in the way you relate to other people. They are reflected in your relationship to your children, to your job, to your friends. You don't change colors like a chameleon when you walk out the door of your house, unless you are playing some kind of false role. The Eros person is just as warm and approachable on the job as during times with his or her children. Such a person enjoys friends and is loyal to them. Secure in his or her own self-image, he or she is not playing games in relationships to others.

The Balanced Ledger

Unless I perceive that what I am giving to a relationship is matched by what I am receiving, my inner system is likely to register an "unbalanced ledger." It is this feeling, if unreleased, which can distort memory of the past and skew expectations for the future, leaving the individual unfulfilled and lonely. Regardless of the kinds of love expectations, the fact that these expectations are rooted in our own human nature and personal experiences makes it prerequisite that some depth sharing is needed if both partners are to have a sense of fairness, balance, and well-being.

People who understand each other and are committed to a relationship can go a long way toward satisfying the human needs even of those with seemingly opposite expectations. A cool and reserved person who has never cultivated intense, emotional relationships may find ways to satisfy a person of great emotional intensity if one, at the same time, is receiving the kind of meaning and companionship that one considers essential to one's own well-being.

There are people who posture in their relationships, trying to appear to be what they are not in order to hold the other person. A self-examination of what one has received and given in the past and what one would receive and give in a love relationship in the future should be sufficient to enable a person to see the untenable position that is likely to follow when one or both persons are attempting to be something they are not in order to hold or develop a relationship.

What may be gained in self-insight from an examination of what I expect to give and to receive in a love relationship? First, I begin to understand more of myself through thinking about what the other one received from me and what it was I gave in return. Am I a person who can both give and receive? Do I place conditions upon this relationship that are difficult for another person to understand? Even when this means that the understanding focuses on what I failed to give, I gain by the understanding. Moreover, the process enables me to articulate what I really am looking for in a relationship with another. If the relationship is considered at more depth, I can see the needs in myself that were rooted in my childhood experiences and then became the hunger and void that made the love relationship so meaningful to me or that made it so lacking in fulfillment.

Perhaps, for the first time, I am aware of the void that was left because my own father and mother were not able to give me parental love. This may have caused me to seek such love from my former spouse, which he (or she) was willing to give until he (or she) became aware that he (or she) was not getting much in return.

True love means a willingness to give in equal measure what I expect to receive.

53

responsible parenting

Parenting is a tough job whether you are doing it alone or are sharing its demands with a partner. There probably has never been a time when it was more difficult to be a parent than today, for we have taught our children that they have the right to question our authority. With all of the other problems you have had to face in your new role as a *single* parent, there may be a temptation at times to feel that the heavy responsibility of parenting is more than you can bear. We know you can do it; you can because you must, and you can do it responsibly. We hope we can give you courage to face what must be faced and to connect you with some resources that are available to help you with the task.

Most of us complain that we didn't have any preparation for becoming a parent; there wasn't any Parenting 101 in even the best of schools. Actually, we did have training, though most of us were not aware that we were getting it.

> Parents get the resources to parent their children because they themselves have been parented with some integrity. If they did not get such parenting—either from biological parents or from some other source (such as a loving community or extended family)—they cannot give it to their children. ("You can't give what you didn't get,". . . .) And throughout their lives, people deprived of parenting will continue to seek it, sometimes even from their own children.[1]

[1] "After Divorce, Children Still Need the Parents," from the *Philadelphia Inquirer* series written by Sharon Nelton, July 11-16, 1976, based on interviews with Dr. Barbara Krasner, Margaret Cotroneo, Dr. Douglas Schoeninger, and Geraldine M. Spark of the Family Psychiatry Department of Eastern Pennsylvania Psychiatric Institute (EPPI) in Philadelphia, where the authors of this book received clinical training.

55

So perhaps the beginning point is for you to think about the kind of parenting you received. Did you have reliable parents on whom you could depend? Consider the style of parenting that was practiced. Who was the disciplinarian and how was punishment administered? What kinds of expectations did your family have for you? Did you feel cheated in any way during those years? Were your parents available to you when you needed them? These questions are important to your understanding of why you relate to your own children as you do. You probably will need to talk with your parents again (if they are living) to understand more fully why they did some of the things they did. You may be able to see their "side" of some actions that have puzzled you or caused you to hold resentments against them far too long. You may want to hear something about the kind of parenting they themselves received in your effort to understand why they acted as they did.

Who Is a "Responsible" Parent?

We can begin by listing the items that are "givens" in what is expected of a parent—to provide food, clothing, shelter, and care for physical needs. Beyond that, in terms of the important human relations, we feel that a child is entitled to

—learn fairness through giving and receiving of fairness among family members.

—parenting from both biological parents.

—have limits set and be held accountable by the parents.

—learn how to trust the world through the family experience.

—own his or her ethnic, racial, and religious heritage.

—make claims upon the parent and hold the parent accountable.

You may be surprised that "love" is not included in the list. While the word love itself does not appear, it is implicit in every one of the items on the list. Tell your children you love them, and then demonstrate what love means by the ways you relate to them. Having received love from you in this way, they will be much more able to give it back—to their parents, their children, and their future spouses.

Fairness

"My basic view," says Dr. Krasner, "is that what we value usually comes from the way significant people have treated us. In the long run, reciprocal fairness is what parents need to teach kids and to give to kids.

I think it is the greatest legacy, the only legacy, we can finally leave."[2]

Each member of the family in which reciprocal fairness is the basis for relationship learns that while he or she will not always come out with what is desired, at least everyone's side will have been considered before the decisions are made. The parent who acknowledges that each child has a right to be considered fairly will have taught the child an invaluable lesson.

This does not mean that *every* family decision requires a period of negotiation, or that the parent should tolerate an extended hassle every time a teenager asks for the car or is asked to sit with a younger child for the evening. It does mean that there can be some leeway on bedtime if the child has a reasonable ground for extension; it does mean that a child will be provided a "why not" when a serious request has to be denied; and it does mean that plans an older child has already worked out will be taken into consideration. The processes of "hearing" and being fair never excuse the parent from exercising the responsibility for parenting by making the critical decisions, but it does call for a family style in which children and parents are free to express themselves in appropriate ways and know that they will be heard.

Parenting by both parents

If both parents are living, it is important that the children have access to both of them. We don't underestimate the problems involved and the cost in terms of emotional drain, but the rewards outweigh the cost. One young woman said,

> My "ex" knows just where to put the needle in. I want to have the children continue to see him whenever possible, but it sure hurts. My kids are preschoolers; so when he writes to them, I have to read the letters. Last week, this "Mr. Wonderful" wrote to them telling them the details of his honeymoon trip. I read the letter to them, and then I went into the bathroom and bawled.
>
> How can I possibly allow them to visit with him now that he has remarried, without worrying about it? He buys them toys galore that they don't need, and it's party time every visit. Meanwhile I sit here with no money except the little support he sends, and have to say no to all the extras the kids want. I'm terrified he'll decide that he wants them now that he is married; and it makes me think I'll take them away somewhere and never let him see them.

Obviously, this man wanted to hurt his former wife by requiring

[2] *Ibid.*

57

that she read about his honeymoon. The problem of the weekend visit is a common one. The custodial parent has the care and responsibility of the children, must provide most of the discipline, must set the limits of behavior, and must endure the pain of having the children spend a great deal of their time longing for a relationship with the other parent. Many custodial parents and many teachers complain that the weekend visit sends the children back home and back to school torn apart emotionally by a parent who tries to cram all of his or her frustration about the parent role into a two-day period.

Often the legal profession does not help with this problem. The legalities of the divorce and the bitterness of property settlement may leave little room for communication between the parents when the legal process is all over. All too few lawyers are convinced of the need for the noncustodial parent to have regular access to the children.

Perhaps the most difficult part of all is the parent who refuses to see the children. For some people, seeing the children on an occasional basis is so painful that they feel that it would be better in the long run for themselves and the children if they were never to see each other.

> My husband simply refuses to see the children. He told me that he would continue to provide for all our needs but that he was trying to forget he had a family. He won't answer my telephone calls, he returns any letter I send to him unopened, and I have no way to let him know that his son is hurting to see him. He is doing poorly in school even though he is capable, and his behavior is getting worse every day.

58

This woman has tried to hold her husband accountable for continuing to parent his children. It could be that she will need to have some help in getting him to realize that the children deserve to have him available to them. But the important thing here is that at least she has tried. Someday when the children ask why their father never visited them, she will be able to say with integrity that she tried, at least, and then she can encourage them to try for themselves.

> My children, a boy, twelve, and a girl, seventeen, have been very deeply affected by their feelings of abandonment, and justly so. My biggest problem now is that the rage they're beginning to express is all directed at me. You know, it's all my fault for causing the sudden departure. In fact, everything that goes awry in their lives is my fault. Perhaps one of these days we as a single parent family can stop rotting from the inside out.

Children find many ways for expressing the rage they feel at having been abandoned. The safest place to direct that rage is at the parent whose love is most dependable.

The longing of a child for the biological parents never ceases. The child continues to hope that somehow the family can be reconstituted. Sometimes the child will engage in elaborate schemes to bring this about, and the parents need to be aware that this may be the occasion for what seems to be bizarre behavior patterns.

When one parent is dead, the surviving parent has the responsibility of keeping alive for the child a true image of what the dead parent was like. The child should not be given a distorted picture of some godlike (goddesslike) creature who never even had bad breath. The child needs to know what the real person was like; what kind of personality he or she had; what music was preferred; what likes and dislikes, favorite foods, and even bad habits he or she had. Then the dead parent is real, and the child can relate to the parent in meaningful ways. The child's self-image is tied to both parents, and he or she needs to be able to make the connection.

Many adoptive parents have experienced the pain of having their child grow up and question them about the biological parents. The newspapers are constantly reporting cases of people spending great sums of money looking for their natural parents. Some adoptive parents find this search threatening and refuse to share with the child any information they may have about the child's parents. Though the process may be painful, these children need to have help in looking for the parents. In the long run they will be able to sort out for themselves the truth of what they have received. They need to be able, when possible, to face their natural parents and have an opportunity to ask why the parents gave them away. The parents have a side, too, and it will help these children to hear that side. If the explanation is inadequate, they will have the opportunity to evaluate it and will not blame the adoptive parents for blocking their search. WHO AM I? is a compelling question for every individual and is inexorably tied to one's biological roots.

After divorce or separation, it is possible for parents to work out an arrangement for both of them to continue to parent their children. The children need to be continually assured that both parents love them; that the children were in no way responsible for the separation; and that although they cannot live together, both parents will be available to them. If one parent is resistant to this kind of "team parenting," then the other parent has to take the initiative to hold him or her accountable. It may require some help, either through another family member or a professional counselor, to facilitate this kind of facing.

One reliable parent is able to parent responsibly. But in some cases—where the noncustodial parent refuses to see the child, lives so far away that he or she is unavailable most of the time, or is dead—the custodial parent will want to find a substitute "parent" who can provide additional adult relationship for the child.

The first suggestion would be to look carefully among members of the extended family. If it is the father who is absent, perhaps a male grandparent on either side would help, perhaps an uncle or a cousin. Tell him what you are trying to do, and try to enlist his help on a regular basis, to take the child/children on special outings or simply make some time available for companionship. There are Big Brother groups in many communities who will provide companionship for boys. Unfortunately, such organizations for girls are less well known. But the same kind of familial possibilities may be explored for an absent mother.

If there are no family members available, you might consider asking for the same kind of help from a friend. If so, and the friend is married, make sure that you discuss the idea with both husband and wife in order to avoid any possibility of misunderstanding what your motives might be. You will also want to make sure that your child/children agree that the persons you will contact would be those with whom they would enjoy spending time.

Limits and accountability

60

To be a parent requires the courage to set limits for the children even when emotionally you want to coddle them and give them only what they want. The single parent is always vulnerable because of the felt need to assure the child that love is constant and that the child will not be abandoned again. Some parents draw back from requiring accountability for fear the child will read this as a withdrawal of love. Whenever a parent finds this too difficult and relinquishes the parental position, the child is robbed of one of the basic rights—the right to be parented. As a result, the child is thrust into the impossible role of acting for the parent ("parentification" of the child), and the child is sent on a vain quest to fill the void, often making demands that are impossible for others to meet or acting in ways that are destructive of others.

During the past twenty years, many people have accepted the theory that it is good if "kids do their own thing," that they will learn from the experience. That kind of thinking has caused a great number of families to subject their children to a different kind of abandonment: psychological abandonment by physically present parents, which leaves the children confused and resentful.

Actually, the greatest love for the child is always expressed through the integrity of parenting that sets reasonable limits for the child and requires accountability from the child. In adult life men and women who think back with satisfaction to their own experiences of being parented are those who had a parent who required something of them, expected responsible behavior from them, and held them to the requirements. In an article in the *Philadelphia Inquirer,* Darrell Sifford reported a conversation with Dr. James L. Framo, professor of psychology at Temple University and family therapist:

> There should be certain non-negotiable limits set by parents of teenagers. . . . On the matters that aren't critical parents can be more flexible and can arrive at rules after discussing them with their teenagers. . . .
>
> In my practice it's rare to see kids in trouble coming from strict parents. Mainly I see the opposite. I see parents not taking a stand with their kids and their kids are doing what they please and sometimes getting into trouble.
>
> I treated one woman, as an adult, and she told me: "You know, my mother never gave a damn what time I came in. If she'd set limits, I'd have fought her, but secretly I'd have been pleased."[3]

Among the issues he found critical and on which parents should not bend, Dr. Framo listed:

> • Making certain that the teenager tells his parents where he will be at all times and that he leaves a telephone number where he can be reached.
>
> • Setting a definite time when the teenager must be back home.
>
> • Ruling out certain "self-destructive" behavior such as heavy drug involvement.[4]

It may seem easier to allow a child to make decisions for himself or herself, to exercise the time-honored dodge of shrugging the shoulders and saying, "Make up your own mind; it's up to you." Such irresponsible behavior by a parent thrusts onto the child a burden he or she is not mature or experienced enough to assume. In the long run the cost to the parent will be great. A twenty-nine-year-old "flower child" said recently,

> When I was a kid, I can remember the terrible arguments my folks used to have. I would hide in my room and turn up the radio so I wouldn't have to hear. I was terrified of what might happen. They finally separated and ended up by getting a

61

---

[3] Darrell Sifford, "Teenagers Want Behavior Limits, Psychologist Says," *Philadelphia Inquirer* (September 30, 1976), Section D, p.1.
    [4] *Ibid.*

divorce. From that time on, my mom was so involved with her life that she was glad when Dad gave me a car and the money to go anywhere I wanted to. They bragged about my independence, but I knew they really just wanted me to go away. They didn't care what I did, so long as I didn't mess up their lives or get in their way.

The words were spoken with difficulty. Having fathered a child in an unsuccessful first marriage, this man was now contemplating divorce from his second wife. He was simply unable to give what he hadn't received from his own parents, and every time the going got rough, he could not face it and took "flight" in one form or another. Both wives had for a time "parented" him, refusing to hold him accountable for his irresponsibility. When they began to make claims on him, he looked for another place to run. Already involved with a third woman, though still living with his second wife, he explained,

> Ginny makes me feel good. She doesn't give me any hassle. I want to have fun and feel comfortable with a woman. She goes wherever I want to go and doesn't get in my way.

The sense of having been cheated in life has a persistent and relentless way of showing up in succeeding generations. In the alchemy of intergenerational dynamics the rage of one generation will manifest itself sooner or later in a succeeding one. The pattern need not repeat itself if individuals can come to terms with relationship distortions, face those who have shortchanged them, and begin to rebalance the relationship.

Experience trust

[Dr. Douglas] Schoeninger says: "The roots of trust are in the family. When you see adult children suddenly grasping that their parents love them, that the parents are able to say that and the children are able to say it to the parents, you see . . . trust. And trust between parents and children . . . generates trust for other relationships."[5]

After the trauma of divorce, separation, or death within a family, it may be necessary to reestablish a capacity for trust in your children. For most children, a stable family is a trustable relationship. When that is taken away, they sometimes become very wary of trusting anyone. The child may feel, *If one parent abandons me, isn't the other one apt to do the same thing?* You can begin to rebuild that trust by constantly reminding your children that they are loved, that you will not abandon them, and that they can count on you in the

---

[5]Nelton, *op. cit.*

future. Probably the loneliest child we have ever seen was a young man of sixteen who, when asked whom he trusted, replied emphatically, "I don't trust no one but me." Abandoned by his mother in early childhood, he had been cruelly abused by his father and had run away from home at the first opportunity. Because he had never experienced a trustable relationship, his attitude was not surprising.

Level with your kids, and let them relearn—if they need to—that they can risk trusting again.

Rootedness

In recent years the black movement has made great strides in helping the black population in this country appreciate its cultural roots. With slogans such as "Black Is Beautiful" to encourage them, more and more people are willing to affirm their heritage rather than deny it as they have in the past. The same should be true for every individual. Each of us is a combination of ethnic, racial, religious, and family characteristics and traditions that help to make us unique. Certainly every child wants to feel an "alikeness" with his or her peers, but there is strength in our differences; and in affirming all of those rootages, the individual can come to have an increased sense of personal worth.

This rootedness can best be given importance in the family. We need to share with our children what knowledge we have of our ancestry. We can do this in many ways: by enlisting the whole family in a search of records to make up a "family tree"; with the celebration of religious and national holidays; and even in the style of clothing we wear or the foods we prepare for special occasions. All of these efforts will help our children to appreciate and enrich our heritage, and give them an increased sense of belongingness.

63

Claiming and accountability

We hear a great many people saying, "I can't ask my parents to help me. They have had enough trouble in their lifetime. I have to protect them." In taking that attitude, you can shut off the most important resource you have, and you are denying your parent the opportunity to continue to be needed in your life. The need for parenting does not cease at some magical age. It varies over a lifetime and may indeed reverse itself to allow the child to do the parenting. The diagram on the next page shows this change in relationship of parents and children in a schematic way. In any particular relationship the changes will not follow such straight-line patterns, and the reversal may not be as extreme as that shown.

During the child's infancy, the parent is almost totally responsible for the child, supplying all of the child's needs as the parent perceives them. As the child grows and is able to communicate with others, the parent gradually allows the child to have more freedom, to make some small decisions for himself or herself. This relinquishing of control by the parent continues to increase throughout the growing years of the child, varying from child to child, according to the parent's judgment of the child's ability to make decisions. The reversed arrows in the left-hand side of the diagram indicate those occasions of special stress when the parent may call upon the child for guidance or allow the child complete control for a brief period of time.

By the time the child reaches maturity, ideally the parent will have prepared the child to be an independent, self-confident individual. (It must be noted that all or almost all children will push against the parental control throughout their growing years, constantly testing the parent's determination to set limits and to hold the child accountable.)

Throughout the adult years of life, the individual calls upon the parent for guidance in special situations and provides assistance to the parents during times of their special need.

When the parent reaches the final stages of life, it becomes the adult child's responsibility to provide parenting to his or her aged parents and possibly at last to balance the ledger of relationship by assuming almost complete control of a parent who is no longer physically or mentally able to care for himself or herself. As with the growing child, the declining parent will push against this kind of control, testing the authority of the parenting adult child.

This pattern of relationship is seldom followed precisely, but it does demonstrate a continuum of long-term parent-child relationship, which is repeated in generation after generation. Obviously, if the child feels that he or she did not receive rightful parenting, he or she will find it difficult to give back what was not received. But for the

64

child who experiences a caring, trustable relationship with the parents, the need to give back will be compelling.

Just as parents have the right and the obligation for holding their children accountable, children have the right to hold their parents accountable—to be able to make claims on them. Parents are responsible to their children because they gave them life, and children are responsible to the parents for the gift of life.

The Child's Adjustment

We often meet newly divorced, widowed, or separated persons who are so devastated by what has happened to them that they fail to understand that the children are going through the same stages of adjustment as the parents. The children will deny that their family is in trouble or that a parent is dead; they will be filled with rage; they will blame the parent whom they feel has abandoned them. And they will mourn the loss of a parent. Grief is experienced by children of separation and divorce just as much as by those who lose a parent by death. All of these painful adjustment periods need to be understood by you in order that you can help your child get through them without psychological damage.

Children need to know that you hurt, even when you have been the one to initiate a divorce. Broken relationships are painful for all of the people involved, and knowing that their parents feel the pain will give children permission to tell them how they feel.

65

Sometimes, when there has been no real opportunity for dealing with their feelings, children will act out in school. They may take flight in drugs or alcohol or find some other form of escape that will be difficult to deal with. A frantic mother recently called for help with her four teenaged children. Her husband died a year ago. He was a strict disciplinarian, almost to the point of cruelty. The boys admitted that they hated their father, and their mother felt intimidated by him, also. The marriage had been stormy, and his death had brought her some sense of relief. Every member of the family is guilt-ridden. Each of the children is expressing his or her guilt and grief in a different way—minor scrapes with the law, involvement with alcohol and marijuana, and poor school performance. The mother, who was abandoned by her parents at an early age, is simply unable to demand any kind of accountability from her children. The only parenting she ever received was from her husband; and he, too, by dying, has abandoned her. She has run out of energy and is willing to stop trying to save her family from the chaotic life it is now experiencing.

None of the children in this family is really bad. Actually, the children are crying out, through various means, for someone to help them. By behaving in unacceptable ways, they may attract the attention of someone who will provide the guidance they need.

There is a great deal of caring within this family, though at times the members work hard to disguise it. The mother cares deeply about what happens to her children but simply does not know how to go about helping them. At last, willing to face her own lack of skill, she took a courageous step in asking for help. All the family members are now involved in family therapy and are working on identifying the resources within themselves that can be brought together to heal their damaged relationships.

Therapy is not the answer to all distortions of a relationship. It is, however, a useful resource when a family is "stuck" in trying to work out its problems.

Weekend Parenting

One of the stickiest problems faced by single parents is how to find some satisfactory answer to the persistent question, "What can I do with my children on a weekend that will not be so artificial that it will further separate us?"

One good approach is to work with your former spouse in a "team" approach to parenting. Discuss your children's progress, their needs, your future hopes for them. This will give your children a significant example of how adults can work out tough issues. They will then not be tempted to try to split you apart on decisions, causing further difficulties. Children soon learn that if they can be successful in splitting your decisions, they will be able to get something they would not otherwise have had.

If you are able to work as a team, the children will not have to deny their loyalty to either one of you. They will not have to choose sides between two people they love; rather, they will feel comfortable enough to move back and forth between you without apology or discomfort.

You also need to consider what arrangement for visitation is the least disruptive of the child's normal life. For example, many children are involved in group activities on a weekend, such as scouting, sports, or religious activities. If a visit with the noncustodial parent means that the child is denied the opportunity to participate in these activities, he or she will sooner or later resent it and feel as if the visit is some kind of punishment, no matter how much the child longs for the relationship. If at all possible, arrange to accommodate these activities by picking up the child afterwards or, better still, by participating with the child either actively or as an interested observer.

When possible, one of the interesting things you can do with your children is to let them see where you work. You might take them to work with you for a short time, if this is appropriate. It is hard for children to picture what it's like for you when you are not living with the family. For some children, it is a thrill to have you introduce them to your co-workers and see your pride in them. Above all, try to find things to do with them that are not simply entertainment. BE a parent. Don't try to buy their affection by spending a lot of money for things they don't really need. Don't get them so excited by frantic activity that it will be hard for them to calm down when they go home. Spend time, quality time, with them. Just take an opportunity to watch something together on TV (although there is little communication with this), or share something with them that you have saved for the visit—even if it is no more than a cartoon you found in a magazine. This will let them know that you are thinking about them when you are apart. Be alert for things in newspapers or magazines that you think they would enjoy, and drop these in the mail to them with a note. Children love to receive mail, and the message is clear that you are remembering them when they receive something from you in the mail.

Some parents have deliberately found a new hobby that they can share with their children on weekend visits. This can be as simple as planting a small garden, building a bookcase, or learning to cook something new.

67

The matter of schoolwork is sometimes a problem. Custodial parents and teachers often complain that the noncustodial parent, even the most cooperative one, may cause unneeded anxieties in a child when the parent insists on helping the child with homework on a weekend visit. Some suggested activities for these visits, called "Take-Me-Alongs," are included in the Appendix and will give you an idea of the kinds of things you could do with your child which would be supportive of his or her classroom work but would not interfere with it. A custodial parent might show these samples to the child's teacher, and ask that he or she help prepare or suggest some appropriate "Take Me Alongs" for your child. Then when the child comes for a visit, some of these can be brought along; and you can have a simple, yet instructive, activity together. The samples given are scaled to the elementary school child. Children at the secondary level may be working on extended projects with which you can help in some way.

Also, older children or teenagers might be asked to work out some plans for a visit, suggesting things he or she would enjoy doing with the parent.

ABOVE ALL, keep in mind the following DOS and DON'TS:

DO	DON'T
Demonstrate your continuing concern for your child.	Quiz your child about the activities or companions of your "ex."
Make it easy for the child to love you AND the other parent.	Ask him or her to carry the messages which you are unwilling to deliver yourself.
Be responsible, not allowing the child to behave outrageously.	Spend your precious hours together scapegoating your former spouse.
Keep on schedule, picking up the child on time and returning at the agreed-upon time.	

YOU CAN'T BE BOTH MOTHER AND FATHER TO YOUR CHILDREN, BUT YOU CAN BE PARENT!

Questions Single Parents Ask

My children were all very young when my husband died, and they can hardly remember him. How can I help them?

Why not put together a scrapbook with pictures you have of your husband? Write a paragraph or two about each picture, explaining where and when it was taken.

Have some of his relatives write what they remember about his early childhood and youth, little stories that give indications of his faults and virtues, likes and dislikes, sports he enjoyed, etc. Make him seem like a real person, one they can relate to and enjoy.

My wife left me to live with another man. How can I allow my children to visit her under the circumstances?

She is their mother, and that bond is one which can never be broken. She has every right to see them and parent them, and the children need to see her. That her values are different from yours does not give you the right to deny them the continuing relationship.

My eight-year-old daughter clings to every man who comes to visit me, and I am embarrassed. My male friends are put off by this—I think they are scared I'm hearing wedding bells on the first date. Her own father refuses to see her.

She is longing for a relationship with her father. You have to make every effort to try to hold him accountable for parenting her, and you may need some help to do this. Have you access to a member of his family who might intervene? You must make the effort; and if you are unsuccessful, someday perhaps you can encourage her to try for herself.

As for your male friends, you should let them know before they come that this may happen, and then you can firmly limit her clinging. If, however, the male friends are put off by the needs of an eight-year-old child, I wonder about your choice of companionship.

I have two sons, ages eighteen and sixteen. Both of them are into drugs, and I cannot handle it. They remind me that their father is an alcoholic every time I try to talk to them about the drugs.

Where do you stand on drugs? (You didn't mention what kinds of drugs they are using.) How firm is your position? We once advised a woman who was struggling with the same problem with which you are that if she really meant that she would not permit her children to smoke marijuana in the house, she should tell them so and be prepared for the consequences. They may decide to live elsewhere. That will be hard for you; and so you want to be sure how firmly you oppose the use of whatever drug they are using.

You might also want to contact your local drug rehabilitation center to get their advice on how to handle it. If you are unsure where it is, call the local police; they will tell you without asking many questions. If no such center is nearby, write or telephone the National Clearinghouse for Drug Abuse Information, 11400 Rockville Pike, Rockwall Building, Room 110, Rockville, MD 20850. Phone: 301-443-6500

69

Two of my children visit their father regularly, but the oldest one refuses to go. She gets physically ill when I try to force it. If she doesn't go, my "ex" will haul me into court.

Children will do anything to protect their parents. It appears that this child is feeling the need to protect you, and her going to visit this other parent may be seen by her as disloyalty to you. You have to encourage her to go; let her know you have plans for the time she is away, emphasizing that you will not be lonely. This may be hard, but you will help her if you are firm. No doubt she wants to go but is torn apart by her guilt. If this does not work, you may need to get some professional help for the child, and we would always opt for involving the whole family if therapy is the only answer.

NOTE: Much of the philosophy reflected in this chapter is based on the work of Ivan Boszormenyi-Nagy and Geraldine M. Spark, *Invisible Loyalties* (Harper & Row, Publishers, 1973) and their colleagues at the Family Psychiatry Department of Eastern Pennsylvania Psychiatric Institute.

The families cited have been seen in seminars or in private family consultation by the authors. Names and situations have been altered only for the protection of identity.

70

realistic goals

[Virginia's] power of sinking her ambition, and even her identity, into the activities of the man was deeply interwoven with all that was essential and permanent in her soul. Her keenest joys, as well as her sharpest sorrows, had never belonged to herself, but to others. It was doubtful, indeed, if, since the day of her marriage, she had been profoundly moved by any feeling which was centred merely in a personal desire. She had wanted things for Oliver and for the children, but for herself there had been no separate existence apart from them.[1]

One of the most difficult transitions, particularly for those who have been married for several years, is learning to say "I" rather than "we." The unlearning of vocabulary that indicated marriage is as difficult as learning it in the first place. The difference is that there is, for most people, the pain of the reminder that one is no longer coupled. There is also the realization that saying "I" can be much more difficult.

When I was married, if someone called and invited us for a social event that I really wanted to avoid, I could always say that my wife had already made an engagement for that date and then express our regrets. Now, there's no one else for me to lay it on. It was really hard for me to have the guts to say no, and for a while I just avoided it by letting other people plan my life for me.

In fact, one of the most common concerns of the newly singled is their realization that their own identity had been completely submerged in their mate's. This is, of course, more common for women than men.

[1] Ellen Glasgow, *Virginia* (New York: Doubleday & Company, Inc., 1929), p. 426.

71

In fact it may have been the cause of a divorce. The women's movement has raised the consciousness of many women and caused them to move toward establishing their own identity. That sudden change from submission to assertiveness can be very threatening for a man who has become accustomed to a wife whose life is defined in terms of his ambitions, his personal and professional goals. The change is sometimes seen as an indication that the wife no longer loves him. Why else would she be insisting on her own goals?

Saying "I" sometimes takes courage. It is much easier to say "they" or "you" and thereby avoid revealing yourself. On the other hand, if you can learn to state your own feelings without scapegoating someone else, you will have taken a real step forward in rebalancing some of your relationships, including those with your children.

Where Am I Going?

For the single parent who has recovered from the initial shock of a broken relationship, it is important to begin looking for some new goals in life. Even if you are still in the process of recovery, this can be a time of valuable self-examination.

In one sense, you have an opportunity that comes only to those who have experienced some dramatic change in their lives. Whether you chose it or not, you have a new life-style. We hear many singles saying, "My life is over. I had invested so much in my marriage that I can't think of anything for me. I'm going to live only for my kids from now on." That's a pretty heavy burden to put on your children, and it surely will not help them in their own recovery process. They need to have you looking forward, not backward. They need to have you demonstrate for them that life goes on in spite of the pain that has to be borne. You can help them best by having some interests of your own that make you more interesting to them as well as to others.

That does not mean that you center all of your efforts on yourself without regard to your children. But they have to learn to live their own lives. Sooner or later they will need to move away from you, and they will be better able to do it if you are making a life for yourself.

> "Cheshire, Puss, would you tell me please, which way I ought to go from here?" asked Alice.
> "That depends on where you want to get to," he replied.
> "I don't much care where," said Alice.
> "Then it doesn't matter which way you go," said the Cat.

Planning life goals can be done in much the same way that one plans for a trip in a step-by-step process that takes into account all of the factors that have to be considered, including the possibility of some disappointments or some detours along the way.

How Much Time Do I Have?

How much of your life is yet to be lived? Obviously, that is a question that cannot be answered precisely, but there are some facts about life expectancy that may give you an idea. Each year the U.S. Census Bureau publishes a life-expectancy chart. The prediction changes from year to year, depending on the actual experience of the population. A recent one looked something like this:

EXPECTATION OF LIFE IN AMERICA: 1971[2]
Source: U.S. Public Health Service

Age	White		Non-White	
	Male	Female	Male	Female
25	45.4	51.9	39.4	45.9
30	40.8	47.1	35.3	41.3
35	36.1	42.3	31.2	36.9
40	31.6	37.6	27.4	32.7
45	27.2	33.0	23.7	28.6
50	23.0	28.6	20.3	24.8
55	19.2	24.3	17.2	21.2
60	15.8	20.2	14.5	17.9

Let's suppose that you are a white female, aged thirty-five years. According to the prediction, then, you can expect to live 42.3 more years. That's a long time. More than half your life is still ahead of you! Figuring out how you will spend those years requires careful planning.

Where Have I Been?

While you should devote more time to looking forward than to looking backward, the past can be instructive for your future. What have been the good times and the bad times for you? When were the times that made you feel best about what was happening to you? When were the times that you felt things were not going well for you and you were unhappy?

To help you as you recall what life has been like up to now, try this exercise. Take a blank piece of paper and draw a line horizontally across it, which we will call the median. Mark off segments from 0 to 80. It should look something like this:

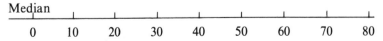

Median

```
   0    10    20    30    40    50    60    70    80
```

[2] Abstracted from *The Official Associated Press Almanac 1975* (Maplewood, N.J.: Hammond Almanac Inc., 1974), p. 247.

Next, draw a stick figure of yourself at the point on the scale which is nearest your age. (Nobody else needs to see your drawing; so let's be honest this time and put it at the right age!) Next, beginning at the left-hand side of the scale, with 0 representing your birth, draw a line from as far back as you can remember which will indicate how you feel your life has gone up to now. That is, we all have highs and lows—times when happiness is intense and times when we feel we're having a really rotten time. For example, a lifeline might look something like this:

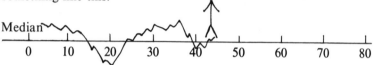

Interpreting our example, you can see that this person, whom we'll call Janice, felt she had a very happy childhood, up to the age of ten. The sudden drop in the line indicates the sense of abandonment she felt when her father left the family. The next few years were rough for her. Gradually, however, she felt better about what was happening, until at the age of twenty, she met and married the man of her dreams.

Janice had entered college and completed two years when she decided to get married. Although she had hoped to have a career, finding a husband who loved and protected her was much more attractive. She gave up her education and within a few years' time had three children. Each of them made her feel more needed, and each time she indicates a sense of elation and fulfillment at the time of each birth. By the age of thirty-five, she began to sense that her marriage was turning sour. Her husband spent more and more time away from home and was totally engrossed in his career. Their communication was poor; they never seemed to have anything in common to talk about. They argued, and the children sensed rather than knew of the impending breakup. When it came, she was devastated. She had devoted her whole being to the home and family, and once again she experienced abandonment.

That was three years ago, however, and now she feels that her life is beginning to improve. At forty-two, Janice is faced with beginning again and is looking forward to how she will cope with the future.

Maybe your lifeline has fewer ups and downs than this one, or perhaps the swing from highs to lows is not as abrupt as our example. Stop the solid line at the point where your stick figure appears.

Look at the line and think about what it represents. There have been good times and bad times. Where are you now? Where do you

74

want to be in ten years, in twenty years? Project a dotted line from where you left off. What direction do you want it to go?

Unless you are a most pessimistic person, you no doubt will project the line in an upward direction. Even if you feel that with the rotten luck you've been having, your life may not be that way, probably you hope that from now on you will continue in an upward movement. Realistically, we know that the movement toward self-fulfillment is never in a straight line, or, at least, rarely is it. There will be some setbacks along the way, but keeping the vision of the goal is a great help in reaching it.

Who Will Go Along?

This journey that you are projecting will certainly have some other passengers involved. You cannot plan for your future without giving regard to the persons for whom you are responsible. You will want to make sure that they are given full consideration. If you are looking forward to some new career (either out of necessity or desire), what part of your planning will involve them? Can they help with some of the decisions that have to be made? Will your plans be feasible in light of your obligation to them? Are there ways they can assist you? A lot will depend on their ages, of course, and their willingness to be involved in your planning process. Are other people going to be involved in caring for the children? *Where do they (the children, the others) want to go?*

Who Can Help Me Plan the Trip?

We have already mentioned some of the people who will be involved in the planning (the "others" involved and the vocational guidance groups), but there are also other sources of help, some professional as well as some nonprofessional. This is one of the times we spoke of in chapter one when you need to tap the resources that are available to you—they are the tools with which you are enabled to do your job more efficiently. You may wish to talk over your goals with a friend whom you trust, your parents or other close relatives, your minister, priest, or rabbi, or the guidance staff at your children's school. The last can help you assess the impact of change on your children. The sources of help in any community are numerous and

75

available to you, once you have decided on your goals. Maybe your goals are modest enough that you don't need any outside help; but if you do, seek it out. Another resource in your community is the library. Look in the "Subject" card catalog for books and articles having to do with careers or life planning.

Many women's groups have money, counseling, support, and job placement services for women, particularly women who want to move upward in their jobs or who are returning to the job market after a long absence.

What Is My Destination?

When you have decided what your hopes and dreams and needs are and are willing to state them clearly, write them down for future reference. Certainly you may change your mind several times through this process, but the fact that you are actively seeking some kinds of objectives will at least get you moving toward something. There may be more than one goal that you have in mind; so put all of them on your list. Then decide which ones are short-range and which are long-range. Your list might look something like this:

1. I have to have a job.
2. I would like to continue my education.
3. I want to do a good job of raising my kids.
4. I'd like to get married again.
5. I want to improve my appearance.

The next step is to settle on some priorities. Rearrange the list in order of the importance of the items to you. This does not assume that you can't achieve all of the things on the list, but some of them will have more urgency than others. (The very use of the term "have to" in the list above seems to indicate priority because of necessity.) Now you are ready to begin making these things happen.

Let's suppose that you have decided that you must get a job because of financial difficulties; so that has to be your first priority. Obviously, you do not have to stop working on all the other things on the list. Some people are doing all five things at the same time, but for most of us that would be too big an order. But there is certainly no reason why one could not aim for success right away with items one and five above.

What equipment do I have? What do I need?

If you are going back to work after a long absence, if you have never worked, or if you have decided to think about a change of vocation—in any case, if a career is in your future—you will want to do some kind of assessment of the skills and experience you have to offer a future employer.

A vocational aptitude test is sometimes useful, particularly if you have never had one or if it has been a long time since you did. These tests usually are available at your state employment office or through a local college or university. A few telephone calls will put you in touch with the right place. In calling a university or college, ask for the guidance department or career planning center.

Even if you are really happy with your vocation and have not been interested in a new field, you may want to consider a change of job for any one of several reasons, such as (1) you need to have a higher income than your present opportunities will provide; (2) you want to get away from the people who know your marital situation, for you are uncomfortable with them now. In this case, you have the advantage of time—you can go about relocating in a less frenetic way and wait for just the right opportunity to come along. It won't drop in your lap, however. In all probability you will have to be alert and active in seeking an opening. Watch the classified ads in your local newspaper; contact the placement service of your college (if you are a college graduate). Sometimes union or professional organization offices have lists of openings. You can let a few trusted friends know that you are looking, or you can visit some employment agencies. All of these sources will protect you by not contacting your present employer if you ask them not to do so.

77

You will need to have a decent résumé prepared to present to a prospective employer. A sample résumé is included in Appendix C, with a full explanation of what you will want to put on your own.

The career planning center may have indicated that you have to have more training for the job you would like to hold. Now your choice is either to get the training and delay your employment until you have completed the training or to take a lesser position and try to get the training during your off hours. Your economic needs may make that decision for you, although you might be able to borrow the money you need to keep your family together while you get the training you must have.

What does it cost?

That depends. If you are on welfare, some states provide financial support for a welfare recipient to get the necessary training needed to become employable. Some colleges give financial help to persons who are going back to school after a long absence. Some employers provide continuing education funds in order to help their employees upgrade their skills. Some families are willing to support even their adult children in educational efforts. Try whichever of these possibilities that apply to your own situation. Remember that some of the state- or county-owned colleges offer the same courses at a much lower tuition rate than the private institutions. You will need to prepare a budget for your whole financial picture, add to it the cost of education or training, and then work from there to decide how you are going to get the necessary funds. Be sure not to under- or overestimate the amounts you expect you will need. One of the benefits of preparing this kind of financial summary is that it helps to convince those from whom you seek assistance that you are truly serious and are going about life planning in a systematic way.

What Detours Can I Expect?

One of the greatest problems about life planning is the blockages you may encounter. Ask yourself, "Why not?" and get started on the

goals that you have identified. This way you will begin to uncover any blockage and be able to deal with its reality or unreality. What is stopping you from moving forward?

1. My kids need me.

2. I don't have the money.

3. My mother-in-law thinks I shouldn't.

4. I'm not smart enough.

1. If you feel that you cannot leave your children, then you may have to conclude that perhaps your priorities got out of order. What you are really saying is that no matter what, the children's need for you is the most compelling of all your goals. On the other hand, if

you know that you have no choice but to find a job to survive financially, then you will need to go about investigating the possibilities for responsible care for the children and plan to give them quality time when you are available.

2. We've already suggested some alternatives to being defeated by lack of funds. The question is, Are you willing to pursue a route around this particular block?

3. Why scapegoat your mother-in-law or anyone else? You are an adult and have every right to be making plans for you and your family which are in the best interests of all of you. When your decision is firm in your own mind, you will have to tell your family and in-laws what you have decided to do, enlisting their help if it is available, and then proceed. Sooner or later they will understand your determination and will probably even admire it. If not, the burden will be on their shoulders, not yours. This does not mean that you should cut them out of your planning, but you are no longer a child for whom they can make decisions.

4. Two things could be operative here. Either you have not yet dealt with your own self-image or you have set a goal for yourself which is unrealistic. An "I can't" attitude will certainly lead to failure; and so you should not even try. You might get by with an "I *think* I can" approach, but your chances of success are much greater if you can manage to make your determination show with "I will!"

Maybe you *have* set an unrealistic goal for yourself, and you will need to examine that possibility. For example, a man who had a difficult time in getting through elementary school, hated math, and did poorly in it would surely be tilting at windmills to think that he could be an engineer without a great deal of very, very hard work. If you decide that your goals are unrealistic, renegotiate with yourself and set out for an easier destination, planning to take the advances in small steps.

79

Taking Off

Delaying the first steps will only make them harder. We all know that taking the first step is the most difficult; but once you're on your way, be certain that you are not going to let anything stop you. There will, no doubt, be delays; there will be unforeseen road blocks; you may even have to make some stops along the way. Remember that childhood game we used to play called "May I?" We had to ask permission to take a step. This is no longer necessary (one of the real advantages of being single)—as long as you are able to continue parenting your children in a responsible way, you can move ahead without *permission* from anyone.

1-2-3-4-5-6-7-8-9-10 MAY I?

we used to say.

Now,   you can tell yourself—

TAKE A GIANT STEP

TAKE 2!

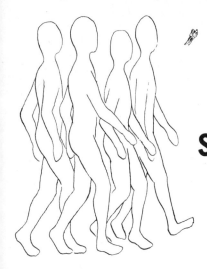

fully alive
in the
singles' world

But how can I pretend to be happy as a single when I really want to get married again?

For me, I don't want ever to get married again, but living alone has really torn me apart. I hate it.

At least two million people each year in the United States alone face this question: "What kind of life am I going to build for myself?" The only reason for mentioning the statistic is that it sometimes helps to know that there are a lot of others in the same boat. Also, it should say to you that there are many experienced people who have made it through and perhaps they have something to say that will help you.

Adjusting to the Single Parent World

The first problem you have to face in making your adjustment is to accept the fact that you are a "single" parent. The label itself takes some getting used to; but your friends, acquaintances, and society generally will use the term often in referring to you. Fortunately, the term no longer carries some of the stigma that used to be attached to it. Today, there are so many single parents that the term no longer seems strange.

The following chart indicates in very general terms three stages of progress most people experience following separation or divorce. Examine the items under the "disruption stage," and see the inhibited, subjective, emotional framework within which many people are living during that period. It is not the optimum time for making long-range decisions. There are too many confusing variables, not the least of which may be the personal variable: Will I be able to see this through? Can I hang together long enough? Experience indicates that jumping immediately toward intimacy as a way to fill the void or responding quickly to the propositions of marriage will lead to another statistic: the failure of a second relationship.

The adjustment stage is the time when things are beginning to move together, when you begin to realize your capacity to cope and to discover the important resources within yourself and among family and friends. It is a stabilizing period. It should lead to the third stage of acceptance of reality and an integration of life forces. This is a period when:

- I am able to relate the way I view myself to the way the groups to which I belong seem to see me.
- I am able to relate the images I have of the way things should be and what I should be with the images people in general seem to have. I am able to work through an understanding of my values and outlook with those of the society around me so that I can give myself affirmation and at the same time be connected with others.
- I am able to view my own life history and appreciate the meaning of the declaring moment of history in which I find myself. I can connect the stream of my life with the person-forming decisions I am to make.
- I can accept myself fully and at the same time "hear" and accept others around me.

Coming to this position is no light task. It requires some hard work and a kind of stability which does not come freely or automatically. One of the ways to get a "reading" on where you are in these stages of development is to ask yourself how accepting you are of what has happened to you and *what you have become.* The fact is you are not the same person you were before your separation from your spouse. If you were to go back to that married state tomorrow, you would be a different person, and so would your mate. You have been doing things for yourself that you never knew you were capable of—perhaps cooking your own meals when you never cooked before, balancing a checkbook, or handling other financial matters.

> I hate to use clichés, but "If I can do it, anyone can." . . . To this day I'm still amazed that I am doing things I never thought I could, like paying the bills or talking to an insurance man. It makes me feel good to find I can do these things.

82

Stages of Adjustment [1]

Following Separation, Divorce, or Death of Spouse

Many people who have worked through the adjustments of being single parents have indicated a movement from one stage to another. The lists below indicate some of the frequently mentioned items.

STAGE I Disruption	STAGE II Adjustment	STAGE III Integration
Loneliness	Efforts to establish self-worth	Develops ability to "pace" oneself
Confusion		
Ego-disruption	Clarification of goals	Selects dating and social experiences that are useful and enjoyable (will prefer to sit home rather than be out for the sake of being out)
Legal, financial pressures	Intensive search for self-identity and a "proper" life-style	
Poor health status	Job security	
Limited financial resources	Health improved	Finds a useful role in the community
Job insecurity	Development of satisfactory social relationships with single people of both sexes	Job security evident
More likely to use people as sexual objects		Prefers sex in love relationship but also may indulge in "sex for the sake of sex"
Relationships frequent and short-lived, or non-existent	Relationships longer lived, may begin to date one or two instead of several	
Children unhappy, more likely to cause problems		Relationships long-term and singular in nature
Communications with spouse difficult or impossible	Sexual involvements without consideration for developing a love relationship	Loves people and uses things
		Children self-reliant
Changed attitudes of family, community, school	Acceptance of community rejection	Financial, legal matters resolved
	Communication with spouse stabilized	Ego intact, may find single life very enjoyable
	Personal appearance may change for the better, creating new image	Ready for remarriage or a semipermanent or permanent relationship or may consider being single the best way to live

83

---

[1]Adapted by permission from a similar form prepared by Willetta Silva-Shadday.

To become fully alive in the singles' world means, first of all, to begin thinking of yourself as "single" and taking some steps to move out into that singles' world. Those who continue to mourn the loss of the couples' world in which they moved before, raging against those actions and events that have stripped them of that world, are not accepting themselves. They are not capable of handling intimate relationships and commitments. Many singles find that they can remain friends with their still-coupled acquaintances but that they must now view them as "daytime friends."

There is no foolproof time line to demonstrate when you will be ready for each of these stages of adjustment. For some there is a rapid movement through the stages and into a form of integration of self and life and society that is creative and enduring. For others, there is a persistent "stuckness" at one point or another so that movement is painfully slow and often requires some outside help.

Even so, movement does not mean that a person gets over the former experiences or that a person does not bear the marks of what has gone on before. But there can be sufficient integration to enable one to live satisfactorily in the singles' world and, by virtue of that, demonstrate the characteristics that are needed for the creation of new and enduring personal relationships. However, until a person can "own" who one is and what has happened to one, that person is not solid company.

84

"It is normal to be a single parent," said a single parent who was speaking before a couples' organization. There was an uneasy ripple in the room. The speaker continued, "It is normal because there are so many of us. It is normal because most single parents go through the stages of mourning and loneliness and rage and come out well adjusted and self-affirming. It is normal because single parents are proving that they can be responsible parents." This concept is harder to accept for those who have never experienced separation in the first place and for those who are still in the first stages of struggling with the hurt and loneliness of a broken relationship. Those who have been through it and have come to accept their own feelings of loss and anger and frustration are those who at depth know that the heart of their normality as a single person is their readiness for intimacy and responsible relationship with others.

Schools, churches, and other institutions are beginning to recognize that they can expect a fourth or a third (in some places, half) of their constituency to be composed of single parent families. There is no way that society can make the judgment stick that children in single parent families are somehow abnormal or that adults carrying the responsibilities of parenting alone are either abnormal or necessarily inadequate. It is important for single parents themselves, for the children of single parent families, for the leaders of institutions, and for society in general to accept the fact that single parent families are here to stay and that they can be strong, growing, supportive families.

There are some advantages of life as a single parent. Discounting some of the baggage brought to this speech, one woman said it straight:

> You won't catch me getting married again. I've had enough of that. I've got everything now. I have all the male companionship I want; and when I don't want it, I can say, "Good night," and he leaves. I am treated with respect and dignity; and if I am not, I can cut the connection. I run my household as I want to. I don't have to nag about mealtimes, about clutter, about anything. I have nobody second-guessing my raising of the kids. It's comforting to know that I could get married if I wanted to, but you're not going to catch me exchanging this life for the privilege of washing somebody's dirty socks.

One man put it in terms of his avocation. He was a businessman but had always aspired to a writing career. Before his wife left him, he had found it necessary to devote almost every spare moment to giving attention to her and to the many things she had planned for them to do together.

> Now I come home at night; and if I want to work, I can cook a light meal, put the dishes away, and settle down to write until I want to go to sleep. Or I can eat out and go to the library if I choose. It would take quite a woman to break up this way of life for me.

Of course, in this instance he did not have the children. He saw them once a week, which helped to account for his feeling of freedom.

A group of singles, discussing the difficulties of their lives alone, turned the subject around and began to think about the advantages. Ideas came slowly at first and then were added with enthusiasm:

—Relief from oppressive "ownership" by spouse
—Freedom to be self-directing
—Stronger individuality
—Time to cultivate individual interests
—More flexibility in schedule
—Freedom to meet a variety of people
—Can develop own taste in foods, home decorating, recreation
—Freedom to pursue serious vocational and avocational interests

85

Some in the group were quick to qualify the list by emphasizing the pressures on the time, energy, and money that limit the freedom of single parents. Then, too, for many the married state is still their goal. Whatever the advantages of being single, they would opt for a good marriage in a minute.

The consideration of advantages is a component of owning what has happened and of the processes of staking out a satisfactory life.

> The load off my back is nothing but relief. I had bottled myself up and sealed me in to protect myself from falling apart. I felt suspended in some kind of preservative, waiting for relief. I always dreaded my husband's coming home. I would never know if he had had a few drinks and would come in loud and abusive, if he would wander in with a vacant air about him, or if he would slouch and be sullen and unresponsive. Some things I could count on—he would want dinner; he would want the kids to be quiet; he would want nothing of me and had nothing to give me. Strapped as I am now with the full responsibility for holding things together for the kids, I feel like I've been let out and I'm free.

A man who had been married for twenty-two years spoke about how the constant bickering, maneuvering, and unpleasantness had shriveled his interests in all aspects of life: his job, his recreation, his reading, his social life, and even interest in life itself. When his wife left him, he said, "It was like stepping out of a subway station at commuting hour into a quiet country meadow with trees and a brook. From years of confusion and tension I found quiet and peace."

The common theme expressed by all these people is that a maturing experience leading to stability and well-being starts with the person being able to affirm himself or herself as a person and to face the particular circumstances that have occurred. It means finding a ground for a pattern of life that can be owned. It means deciding that you are going to have an *intentional* life-style.

Oswald Spengler was fascinated by the ancient Latin saying, *Ducunt Fata volentem; nolentem trahunt* ("The Fates lead the willing man; the unwilling, they drag"). Certainly, it is a common clinical experience to see those who are suffering the deepest human indignity feeling that they are dragged along the course of human existence. It is also common to see those who move toward goals working through the identical circumstances of life and finding strength and meaning in the very process of coping with these circumstances.

What alternatives do you have? You have to make your own list, since generalities can never do justice to your own unique

86

circumstances; but the examples of alternatives that follow may help you to see the range of choices:

—Develop calluses. Get used to the hurt and loneliness and the injustice, and live with it.

—Accept the situation positively as a sacrificial way of honoring the one who is gone.

—Seek relief and release in adult companionship without marriage.

—Deliberately seek remarriage.

—Choose a career, prepare for it, and enter it.

—Adopt a single life-style and give yourself to it wholeheartedly.

—Move in with your parents or any other relatives who will take you in.

The number and variations are almost limitless. The important thing is to see that your choice among such alternatives in itself is important to your own integration. Fundamentally, the patterns of adjustment are conditioned by the kind of person one intends to be. The self-sacrificing, self-deprecating, submissive person who sometimes is characterized as "virtuous" may really be avoiding responsibility by laying guilt on someone else. One who can think of nothing but remarriage may be rushing in that direction to cover up the unfinished business of a former marriage, which may surface later to threaten or destroy the chances of success the second time.

A careful assessment, through self-examination or with professional help, of what is fair may be part of the maturing process itself, which makes possible sound judgment about the future.

87

Dating and Relating

Friends and activities are needed if there is to be a healthy acceptance of the single life-style. Withdrawal can't go on, even though at first it serves to give one breathing time, mourning time, after the finality of the separation is accepted; it has to give way eventually to something else:

For six months I never saw anyone except people I had to work with on the job. I didn't want to see anyone. Frankly, I spent the evenings falling asleep over a newspaper, and I would wake up only in time to go to bed and get ready for another day. This went on until one night I began to realize what was happening to me. I felt as if I were dying. Death was moving in, beginning with the death of any interest in other people. I had no motivation, no incentive. I didn't want to do anything, see anybody. I was really preparing to die at forty-one. I got scared; I started to panic; but I knew I had to do something. I remembered that a friend had told me I should go to the single parent group. I had turned it off fast—that stuff wasn't for me. Now I wondered. I looked them up and decided to try it the next night. I went, and it was the beginning for me—someplace to go, new friends who didn't need an explanation, etc. I was on the way to finding myself again.

You really can't "put it all together" alone. There is no way you can "get your head on straight" through solo exercises and self-discipline and self-control. Somewhere you have to try these ideas out and see if they will work.

No doubt your social contacts have been shifting. Friends you used to enjoy are no longer as interesting to you. Even those who are genuine in inviting you to join them may seem to be condescending. A few things can be received out of their pity and compassion, but lasting and satisfactory friendships are based on both giving and receiving. There comes a time when you feel that these still-coupled friends are "daytime" friends, that nighttime friends are single ones.

Some of these old friends may bring painful reminders of the past that are difficult to handle. There are bound to be awkward moments, since some friends are unwilling to choose sides between you and your former spouse. Someday they may have to; but early in the game, it is difficult for them. The memories of former days are hard; but you will know you have made it, said Fred, "when you can walk down the street and bump into [Marge] and her friends and not wish you could drop through a crack in the sidewalk."

It's hard to start dating again after being married for a number of years. Sometimes you may feel like an adolescent who is starting all over again, or you worry about what everyone is saying:

"What do I tell the children—or the neighbors?"

"Everybody's watching me as if I were cheating." A mother-in-law may say: "It's only been a year. I suppose you can't be alone forever, but I just think what Herbie would say."

Others simply find the problem within themselves. They find themselves constantly comparing the positive and negative points of the date with the former spouse. Realizing the problem, still they say, "I can't help it; I do make the comparisons, and I hate myself for it."

Some of the major problems you may face as you begin to date again might be like those voiced by a group of newly single persons:

—The rules are different from the time I was young. I can't bear having someone ask me to go to bed on the first date.

—Where do you meet anyone to go out with?

—I don't dance and don't drink; so what else is there?

—I really get uptight when a man speaks to me; and I could never start a conversation with a man I don't know.

—I don't mind talking with a woman in the A & P, but it is really hard for me to start a conversation at a party.

—I'm simply too tired after work and taking care of things at home to go out at night.

—I feel guilty about leaving the kids at home with a sitter all the time.

—I'm afraid of what the kids will think.

—I don't want the kids to know I'm having sex.

—I'm afraid the kids will get attached to my date if I continue with the same one; and then if it doesn't work out, it will be the same kind of disappointment for them.

—Frankly, I don't dare trust myself. I was hurt once; that's enough.

—I don't want to hurt my mother-in-law.

—I don't think anyone would really want to go out with me.

—I'm so lonely that I'm afraid I will go all to pieces if someone is nice to me.

89

Obviously, these persons were unsure of their ground. Did they have the right to date? Would anyone want them to go out? Of what values were they sure? Did some of their statements reflect disinterest because of the uncertainty of trying again?

The single parent has to come to the knowledge that the choices are few—either you step out into that singles' world or you probably will remain lonely and single. New relationships are healthy and normal; new relationships need not be distorted; new relationships are no dishonor to the past relationships. Here are a few pointers that might be helpful:

1. Go out with another for what the relationship can provide, not to fill a void left by someone else.

2. Be able to relate your experiences of the past simply and clearly without self-pity, scapegoating, or bitterness. State it once and then leave it alone. No new companion wants to hear about your former mate over and over again.

3. Let your new companions be themselves, and see them as persons in their own right, not making an effort to compare or contrast them with your former spouse.

4. Become interesting yourself and consider what you can give to the person you are dating.

Most people will not find dates by sticking to their accustomed places. Replying to a friend who had complained about a man the friend was dating, Catherine complained,

At least you have someone to fight off. I'd give anything for the chance to say no to sex. It would be a lot better than knowing there isn't anyone who wants to go out with you.

Pressing her, the friend was able to get Catherine to admit that she really hadn't been out looking, hadn't been away from her married friends, had spent most of her time in her apartment, but admitted she wanted to marry again.

The fact is either you step out into the singles' world or your only hope for finding companionship is going to have to be someone else's spouse.

You say you want to meet people? You don't meet them by sticking inside your house and going to the bank and the grocery store. If you don't stir yourself, if you don't go where people are, then don't sit there and say no one's around who could be interested in you. You're hiding. Nobody's going to come and hunt you out. If you mean what you say, then get out where people are.

Many singles who have not dated since the death of their spouse or since the divorce show considerable nervousness when it is suggested that there are single parent groups in every major city. There are both national organizations (Parents Without Partners) and local organizations (Single Parents Society, The Formerly Marrieds, etc.), YMCA, or church-related groups. Many of these groups have discussions followed by refreshments and dancing. Some have strictly dancing and social time, with no discussions of a formal nature. Near the larger cities singles' activities are available every night of the week. Some of them provide group trips, musicals, plays, picnics, dances, activities for families, and camping for children. An increasing number of churches and synagogues are providing attractive activities, study groups, and social events where the formerly married can meet each other at levels that can make enduring relationships possible. Most pastors, priests, and rabbis know where these groups are functioning in their local communities. Often, these events are sponsored by groups of churches and synagogues.

What About the Children?

If you have children, of any age, can you date? What about teenagers, or older, even married children— what if they are critical? Will the young children, preschool or elementary age, feel threatened and hurt?

A troubled mother said, "Sue is four, and she went into a fit of crying when I started to go out; she begged me not to leave her." The sitter was standing by helplessly, and so was the date. "I didn't know what to do. I finally left, hoping the sitter would be able to calm Sue down; but I still felt guilty. Would it be better for me to skip dating for a year or two until Sue is old enough to understand?"

The answer had to be, unequivocally, no. It is important to understand why Sue is feeling threatened and to do something about it. It was found that the father in this case had abandoned the family and Sue had been very close to him. It became clear that Sue was feeling insecure, gripped by fear that her mother, too, might go away and not come back.

91

Certainly there is primary responsibility to Sue. She does need to have security and a basis for trust. This does not mean that dating must be ruled out. Far from it. It does mean that the mother must explain clearly and unemotionally that she is going out for the evening and that this is normal and important to her. Mother will be going out from time to time with adult friends, both women and men. But Sue is loved; is cared for, and Mother will come back. The responsible parent must find ways to let the child know what to expect, how long the parent expects to be away. In doing so, the child will learn that the parent, not the child, is the one who makes the decision, but that the child is loved and will be cared for while the parent is away.

Those who attempt to "protect" their children by misleading them, evading them, hiding from them, have the worst time. Acting firmly and calmly, with openness and honesty, is the only way to enable the child to overcome the anxiety about being abandoned. Deceit is a devastating signal that a parent cannot be trusted.

A date may well represent competition for a parent's attention, and the child may try any number of ways to test the parent's loyalty. This may take the form of feigned illness (or, in some cases, actual physical illness), tantrums, clinging to the parent, etc. Don't panic in these situations; simply tell the child firmly what you are planning to do. If the child is really ill, of course, you will have to decide whether the sitter is capable of taking care of the child and whether medical attention is necessary.

The date may also represent to the child a person who is taking the place of a parent he or she is still hoping will return, and therefore someone who should be discouraged from coming.

If the parent remains sensitive and responsive to what is going on, the child may learn the important foundation for future development, namely, that a parent can be trusted to love and care for him or her and that the child cannot make the decisions for the adult. In no case should the child be allowed to "give permission" for the parent to go out with adult friends.

What About Sex Between Consenting Adults?

The need for sex and the use and misuse of sex are not eliminated just because a person no longer has a marriage partner. Sex is a valid human experience of intimacy, rooted in depth needs that are basic to self-concept and interpersonal confidence. The sex urge is real and should be seen as part of the personal resources an individual brings into human relations.

The sex urge is often abused by separated, divorced, and widowed people who simply cannot stand the void that has been left by the loss of the partner. Instead of dealing with their own grief, or in some cases guilt, many of these people attempt to cover the void by compulsive bed hopping. Still others try to hide the void by assuming a virtuous attitude of "Don't touch me; don't even look at me." Both men and women who are experienced in exploiting others who are sexually vulnerable see both of these put-ons quickly. They recognize the emptiness that makes the person vulnerable.

For most people, the self-image is struck a devastating blow when a partner leaves, especially if a third party is involved. One woman put it this way:

> It wouldn't have been so bad if he had run off with someone ten years younger and with all the right measurements—I could understand that. But no, he had to shack up with a tramp who's my age but looks older and is twenty pounds heavier. It makes me wonder what's gone wrong with me.

The harder the blow, the more apt the abandoned spouse is to take some exceptional action to strike back. This "striking back" can show up in several forms—some prove that they still "have it" by having several sex partners in rapid succession or by inviting a relationship with a much younger mate. Others take an uptight, inflexible stand, saying, "I'll never have sex with anyone again." Either of these directions is apt to be an evasion to protect one from having to face the grief or the guilt or the loss of self-esteem.

The need for sex is multileveled. There are physical stimulations and tensions that may appear to be involuntary and call for physical release or willful denial. An old Michigan farmer told his son, "When you feel like that, exercise a lot, eat leaner, and take a cold shower." Most people know that a physical explanation and a physical release represent oversimplification. Nervous tension, mental imagery, personal security, and interpersonal relations have much to do with sexual arousal and fulfillment. The experience of the adolescent with "wet dreams" is a case in point. The advice of the farmer is relevant; but the need of the adolescent for recognition, to belong, to be somebody in someone's eyes, is also relevant.

One unmarried woman in her early twenties was explaining about her pregnancy. She said, "I knew I hadn't taken my pill; I knew I didn't want to be pregnant; but it was the night before my comprehensive exams for my degree, and I was in such a state of mind that I said, 'Oh, what the hell,' and I let go."

Another woman put it bluntly: "If it were a matter of relieving my physical tensions or even my nervous tensions, it would be simple—I'd masturbate. That would be easier, cheaper, and much less complicated. But it isn't all that easy to find someone you can give yourself to, and that is what I long for in sexual relations."

The widespread popularity of "adult stores" which operate in defiance of the laws of many communities illustrate the role of mind and imagination, dreaming and daydreaming in sexual arousal. The market is attractive to those who would want a vicarious thrill out of peering at the sex act of persons they neither know nor care about. This kind of vulgarizing of sexual stimulation can lead to the loss of the capacity for either self-acceptance or love.

Sexual intercourse is the ultimate symbol of intimacy and depth relationship, and most formerly married people long for a restoration of that kind of "belongingness." The fundamental idea that it is not good for human beings to live alone is imbedded in the creation stories. That inner longing for intimacy and relationship is real and provides the structure for understanding the physical manifestations of the sex act.

Can the sex urge be sublimated, put off, or denied? Obviously,

93

the answer is yes. Men and women have been separated without sex for long periods of time for any number of reasons—prolonged travel, surgery, accidents, or even mutual commitment to abstinence. We all know of healthy adults, both men and women, who practice lifetime chastity in connection with religious vows and other commitments.

It does not follow, however, that all abstinence is automatically good or healthy. There can be bad reasons for refusing to own one's sexual needs, such as an evasion of issues that need to be faced. The fear of sex, the rejection of sex as "dirty, repulsive, and animallike" may be rooted in traumatic childhood experiences or relational deprivation in the primary family. This attitude may have been a negative factor in the former marriage and may remain a factor in adjustment to the single life.

Responsibility and accountability are important parts of sexual intimacy; and, therefore, sex is not a suitable diversion merely to help one "forget the past" or to "fill the void." That may be the purpose of one of the partners, but the expectation of the other may be entirely different, and this is a factor that needs to be recognized.

Responsible and accountable experiences are best supported in the marriage relationship, even though the abuses of sex may take place within marriage as well as outside. A large percentage of the single parents we know have established serious standards for themselves for experiencing the intimacy of sexual relationships without considering remarriage. Some insist on a relatively long-term relationship with one partner; others require the framework of love and understanding; practically all of them reject the various forms of promiscuous love. One woman who has struggled to integrate her religious beliefs and values with her life goals and experiences summed it up:

> I've changed my attitude on sex. I want and need to have deep human companionship. So long as I was safely married, I could afford to take a stand for sex in marriage only. Even after my husband left, I continued the socially correct attitudes about sex. But after two years of making it alone, feeling good about the way I had put my life together, managing to get my values and my personal needs back together, I began to look at it differently. Why should I wait until I am over the hill to find the level of relationship I never had in my marriage? I'm not talking about running around doing "one-night stands"; I want a deep relationship, and that will involve sex. If I ever do get married again, it will be because I remain human and alive and know the meaning of giving myself completely and freely to another.

Realistically, what are the alternatives regarding sex for the man or woman who is separated, divorced, or widowed?

—Abstinence from sex outside of marriage.

—Sex with a partner, provided it is a continuing relationship with accountability being a principle for both.

—Promiscuous sexual activity—with whomever one feels comfortable and wherever there is mutual desire.

—Buying or forcing sex even with relatively reluctant partners.

Whatever alternative you choose, it is important that your choice reflect your own beliefs and values and goals in life. This is not to imply that at a high moment of sexual desire you will be able to have a philosophical discussion, but rather it is to urge you to think about where and who you are and what you want out of life before that moment arrives.

You will want to consider what is fair both to you and to the other party. It is not enough to consider what is OK for yourself alone, since responsible relationships are based on what is OK for both persons. Much suffering and personal damage are done by people who feel no personal problem with casual sex and assume it is the same for anyone else who consents to sexual intercourse. Accountability is not only to oneself but to the other and to those who are not immediately involved but who are affected by your actions.

95

Sex is being talked about more openly, but for some formerly married people the level of sexual activity that is prevalent in the singles' world comes as a shock. One woman reported that she hadn't yet reached the middle of the dance floor with the first partner she had at a singles' dance before she was asked to go to bed. It is just as shocking to some men who are newly singled to find that the women they date are expecting sex on the first date. Some report that they ask right away because they feel it is expected of them. One woman told us,

> My friends had urged me to go out, and finally I did accept a date for dinner. We were obviously not heading for the restaurant he named, and when I asked where we were going, he said, "I thought we would go to my apartment and get the sex out of the way so we wouldn't be nervous all through dinner."

This woman said, "No thanks." Others who heard her explaining this incident felt that the man's idea was perfectly reasonable. Sexual mores in the United States are changing rapidly. There are whole apartment complexes that cater primarily to couples who live together for a year or longer in a style that is open and quite satisfactory to them. Many older couples live together without marriage, often because it protects their financial benefits.

Most formerly married people are acquainted with those friends who are eager to help the "poor, sexually deprived" people. It comes as a shock when friends in an apparently stable marriage offer this kind of service to those they consider to be hurting for sex. Usually, however, this kind of person will disappear upon hearing a firm, "No." Any other answer is loaded with the possibility for trouble.

Some single parents affirm that they find it possible to date without having sex. Others maintain that sex is a natural relationship that can happen when there is mutual readiness but should not be indulged in when either person has reservations or guilt feelings. Still others say that the discussion has no meaning for them because they have never been asked and would have no idea how they might react if they were asked.

We believe it is imperative for the present and for the future that the sex experience be bound by depth relationship, but it is not our purpose here to "wipe you out" because you do not agree. We would only urge you to consider carefully the meaning of sex in your life.

Most children know what is going on between parents; and in the case of a single parent, they are aware of what is happening, also. This is not confined to middle adolescent years; it includes children of much younger ages. Many of them have a rather detailed knowledge of the adult's sexual activity.

96

There was a time when adults thought that children knew only what they had been told about sex; but in this age, we have to be aware that children know a great deal of what has gone on behind the closed doors. Even at the junior high school level, knowledge about sex is comprehensive, from firsthand experience or through reports from others.

Despite this knowledge among their peers, children still learn their standards and inner direction regarding sexual relations primarily from their experience within their own families. The way adults meet their needs for sexual intercourse becomes the primary teacher of what is permissible, if not normative, for the teenage children. It is very difficult to apply a double standard of sexual freedom for the single adult and postponement for the single young adult.

It will be a loving gift to your children if you can provide them with a clear understanding of the sexual relationship as an ultimate experience in human intimacy, around which sound and enduring relationships can grow.

remarriage
without regret

We recognize that there are many people who elect to remain single, but four out of five formerly married persons, according to the national statistics, will marry again. Those who are considering remarriage should commit themselves to working at it so that they will experience that joy and fulfillment they seek and the union of deep significance that is the meaning of marriage.

The national statistics are not too encouraging, however. A far greater percentage of second marriages than first marriages end in failure. The tables show that this is more true of divorced people than of the widowed. But we know from the testimonies of men and women whose second marriages have fallen into trouble that the failures can be avoided if care and effort are taken to maintain the level of giving and receiving in mutual trust that can make a successful marriage. As one person put it,

> We were deeply in love with each other; we knew we were sexually compatible. It wasn't until we began to fall apart that we realized that we had never come to terms with what we really expected of each other. I was shocked when I finally realized that he wanted something of me that, by nature and experience, I could never be. We were stupid not to have seen beyond the romantic love before we were married.

Marriage is the fulfillment of a longing; it is a commitment to a promise that is at once your promise and your partner's promise. In the midst of the transitory elements of this world marriage is the finding of an affinity that promises life and creativity with a future which you want with all your being. Marriage is a covenant between two people in recognition of mutual love in which both are prepared to anticipate and to accept the outcome.

But marriage involves far more than the trust relationship between a man and a woman. It also involves the intricate set of relationships and responsibilities that each brings to the marriage. These may include:

the responsible parenting of the children both may have from a previous marriage;

the primary families of both, with personal and practical needs to be met;

the extended families and the varying levels of mutual concern and dangling obligations;

the commitments both may carry related to their careers and avocational interests;

the belief systems, value commitments, religious affiliations that are significant to each;

physical and mental health considerations that may involve time and money.

98

These only illustrate the kinds of commitments and relationships that each partner brings to the love relationship. To screen these out, to postpone them as matters that in time will take care of themselves is to settle for less than the whole person in the marriage. With people of integrity, matters such as these are registered in the mind and conscience of the individual; they are not merely external ties that can be severed when the marriage takes place.

Marriage must provide room for the dignity and value and even the careers of the respective individuals. There is a need for growing space for the individuals in marriage, so that they may have the independence to contribute equitably to their life together.

Practically everything that has been said applies to all marriages, but there are areas of particular concern in regard to remarriage. The relationship to children has already been mentioned. There are also the memories of the past, and the tendency to compare and contrast. The routines of eating and household chores, decor, habits of rest and entertainment, sports and avocations—all strongly experienced at a former time with a different partner—may give rise to fleeting moments of wondering if the past might be restored. There may be properties and financial assets to consider. The single life-style may have become firmly entrenched as a part of one or both of the persons' routine.

It is pointless to go through all these kinds of sharing and reviewing if there is not a deep commitment of both parties. Even for a perfect "computer-match" of partners, the most beautiful of ceremonies cannot make a marriage without an appreciation of the increased potential of the joined lives. Given that depth of love relationship, there are no problems that cannot be addressed with fairness, and the marriage can be freed to move toward its intended fullness.

The key question is, Do you really want marriage? Are you seeking a level of relationship with another person that can give meaning to marriage, or is it possible that you seek an alliance with another in order to solve other kinds of problems you are facing? Some people choose to get married again as a kind of painkiller, to find relief from the pain of loneliness, damaged ego, or grief. Others seek only to fill a void left by the former experience. Still others look for someone to help take care of the children.

> I married him because I thought the kids needed a father. I had two boys; I felt they needed a man in the house. I didn't think I could discipline them or play with them or get normal work from them. I know now it was a mistake, but I chose a parent for the kids rather than a husband I loved. I really never loved him, although I respected the way he related to the boys. He wanted more, and I didn't have it to give.

99

When the finances are tight, many people begin looking for someone who has enough money so that they won't have to scramble for every dollar the kids need. They are ready to barter: "An attractive wife who will maintain a clean house and will be reasonably interesting, in exchange for the stability of financial support for her and for the family."

What is your real agenda? Marriage is for those who long for another as a completion of their lives and for those who are willing to give full measure to the other as well as to receive. The experience of people who have had the hopes of a good remarriage shattered underlines the danger of exploiting such a marriage to meet other objectives. Seek the full relationship between man and woman that takes into account the relationships and responsibilities each carries. This is the kind of marriage the religious institutions say is ordained of God, and this is the kind that society presents as the public recognition of the joining of two lives.

Expectations of Marriage

Everyone who approaches marriage has expectations of what the relationship is going to be. Too often, those hopes and dreams are vaguely defined in terms of what each of us has recorded consciously or subconsciously about marriage. The marriage relationship we observed between our own parents is probably the strongest influence, although the poets, the novelists, the playwrights, and the mass media have made their impressions on us, also. Men and women preparing for remarriage are sometimes more aware of what they don't want in marriage than what they do want. The focus here is on the "dos."

There is no way that one can be guaranteed that every possibility for avoiding failure will be eliminated. Each of us has seen too many "perfect" marriages fail and too many "hopeless" ones survive to believe that. There is no question, however, that there are some obvious pitfalls that might be avoided if a couple preparing for marriage—for remarriage—would take the time to consider carefully the prospects. Suppose, for example, that you are considering marriage. You know each other very well; you know something of each other's responses; and you are excited and happy about your relationship. You know at least one side of the kind of marriage your "intended" experienced the first time. You should know what obligations are still a part of that former marriage—support of children, visitation with the children, property ownership, etc. In other words, you need to make a serious effort to know what kinds of "baggage" your future wife/husband brings to the marriage.

100

The question is, Have you considered what you expect to get from this marriage, and have you thought about what you expect to give? Facing this question is a vital part of your premarital discussions; and each of you, working separately, should make some kind of list of what you want to get and what you are prepared to give, as you perceive your own needs and the other's. When you have had time to think this through—take a week or two to be sure you have included everything—then you are ready to have a full discussion of what is meant by each of the items on both lists.

Such a listing might be something like the one below, but be sure that your list reflects your own expectations, not someone else's.

What I Expect to Give and to Get

Fulfillment of My Life

I want a relationship with my husband (wife) to be one in which both of us feel that all of our longings and all of our needs are now fully met in what we bring to each other.

[Be sure that you realize what is being said here—if one of you cannot honestly subscribe to this, now is the time to know what needs you expect to have met elsewhere.]

Trust

I want my husband (wife) to believe in me and in my integrity to such a degree that there will never be any question in either of our minds that we can share our deepest emotions, fantasies, desires with each other. I don't want to have to have my motives questioned or fear his (her) jealous reaction if I dance with another person at a party. I would expect to invest the same kind of trust in him (her).

[Does the statement about jealousy reflect a tension point from your first marriage? Would you not want a *little* jealousy to indicate his (her) concern if someone made an obvious "pass" at you?]

Working Together on Mutual Goals

I believe in stated goals, and I want my husband (wife) to work with me on short- and long-range goals so that we will know where we are going. These could be financial or personal goals, but I want him (her) to think about this as much as I do.

101

[This might give you a good opportunity to state what your present goals are for yourself and to see what your partner has in mind for the future. How do your goals mesh with those of your future spouse? Are they compatible?]

Sexual Satisfaction

I would expect my husband (wife) to understand my persistent need for the intimacy of sex. I would be prepared to understand if his (her) need were less intense than my own. I would be willing to try new techniques to improve our sexual rapport.

[Are you talking about sexual intercourse only when you discuss sex? Are there other times you would enjoy intimacy, e.g., touching, caressing, fondling as an indication of physical enjoyment?]

Commitment

I will be fully committed to the marriage, expecting to be

together "until death." I don't expect to give up easily because of little annoyances. I will not abandon my husband (wife), and I expect that he (she) will not abandon me.

[Are there any conditions in which you will abandon the marriage? Do you mean "in sickness and in health" in its broadest sense?]

Accountability

I expect my husband (wife) to hold me accountable for my behavior, and I expect to do the same for him (her). I will not do for him (her) what he (she) should do for himself (herself), and I will expect to be treated in the same way when it comes to important matters.

[Be careful here—you'd better be sure your spouse understands that you are this "liberated." Better define what you mean when you say "what he (she) should do for himself (herself)." He (she) may define that differently.]

Room for Creative Development

102

I want and need to have a husband (wife) who cares enough about me to be concerned about my self-image and self-improvement. I want to give attention to the same things for him (her). This means to me that we seek out opportunities and help work out details for this to be a part of our lives. This may mean that each of us will pursue a career on a full-time basis.

[Do you have an understanding also about responsible child care, household duties, etc., that both of you accept?]

Relationship with Children

I expect to be the most important person in my husband's (wife's) life, and he (she) will be the most important person in mine. I will provide loving care for my spouse's children as well as my own, and I expect that he (she) will do the same. We will agree on our style of parenting and will apply it to all our children.

[The hazards in working out your parenting arrangements will require long consideration.]

Financial Considerations

I expect to share with my spouse a full knowledge of my financial resources, and I expect to know about his (hers). I would prefer a premarital agreement that will protect my children's personal interests in assets from my previous marriage and will also make the same provision for his (her) children. I understand fully what my husband's (wife's) financial obligations are for supporting his (her) children.

[The premarital contract is used more and more often by couples who are marrying for the second time. It is reassuring to the children, particularly teenagers or older children, to know that their interest is not threatened.]

The Little Stuff

I expect that my spouse will scratch my back at the appropriate times (when it itches). I expect he (she) will not scream with pain when my cold feet touch his (hers). In return I will endure his (her) snoring with patience, and his (her) TV viewing without clinched jaw.

[A little showing of humor in such a serious discussion is not inappropriate, it seems to us; and the little stuff needs to be addressed as well as the more important matters.]

Not all of these items may be the matters of most importance to you. But think carefully on what you believe marriage is all about—such thought may be the most important investment of time you have ever made.

103

What About the Children?

What do you visualize for your children in the remarriage? You have to be prepared for your relationships with your children to change as you bring a new spouse into your life. You are bringing the spouse into their lives as well as into your own. No doubt there has been a distinctive adjustment made between you and the children during the time following the absence of your first spouse. Without realizing it fully, you have given more direct, personal attention to the children than you did when there were two parents present. If there were adolescents, one or another of them may have assumed some protective role toward you.

The dynamics are altered sharply when it is clear to the children that you are finding strength, support, love, and companionship in the adult you have brought into the family and that you are expecting them to share their relationships with him or her. By your action you are asking them to readjust—for example, to forbear giving complete attention to you, receiving full attention from you, and giving protective support to you.

Rather than attempting to slow these processes down or trying to deny them, it is best that you devise a plan that can prepare them for these changes and at the same time help them develop the new relationships in the newly constituted family. This is no time for "family-as-usual" attitudes, expecting the children to accept the new adult in the family merely as a replacement for the one that is not there. Not at all. The children need to be involved in the very processes that will lead to the establishment of the new family in which the new member will be in a position to contribute freely from his or her experience and personality.

One couple worked at this task in the following manner:

After talking with both sets of kids before the marriage, we knew we would have to work at the relationships with the children if it was going to be a good marriage. The kids weren't all that enthusiastic about our marriage. We accepted the fact that we would not (actually we could not) dislodge the loyalty of the children from their other natural parents. But it took some doing on our part to figure out how we could operate as stepparents without breaking into the rights of the absent natural parents.

We began to see more clearly, with the help of a family counseling group, that we had the responsibility for working out the rules for the new family and that we had the initiating responsibility for getting this understood and accepted. To do this, we had to listen with fairness; but we also had to be firm and consistent ourselves. We anticipated the time when the children would react to discipline by yelling, "But you aren't my Daddy!" or "You aren't my Mommy!" By thinking of it ahead of time, we found that it was less of a shock than we had at first thought.

We were open with the kids; we brought them in on the rules; we listened to them; we adjusted some of the rules in light of what we heard. We explained what we were doing, and we demonstrated that we intended to be fair to their side. At the same time we made it clear that we intended to implement a fair procedure as a new family composed of parents and stepparents and that while we expected them to remain loyal to their other parents, we also expected them to cooperate in this present family structure.

Our greatest problem was that neither of us had been that firm and self-confident in our previous marriages. It happened that we both had left the parenting to the other partner. The counseling group helped us see that the only way we could make this marriage work would be to find strength in each other and support each other in relation to the children.

As we view it now—and we have a long way to go yet in our parenting—we would have made some changes in our approach to the children if we had it to do over; but by and large we did the right thing, given our situation.

One of the difficult adjustments has to do with the setting of limits for the children and holding them accountable for those limits. Double standards are definitely out. It is impossible to divide the task—she will discipline her children, and he will discipline his. The new family has to set rules and limits that apply to the entire family, of course taking into account the differences in ages and other factors. The fastest way and the most effective way for the new spouse to come into the dynamics of the family is through the total involvement of the family in setting up the rules and limits that will govern the conduct of the family in the future. It should be clear that both parents are expecting accountability from the children.

Such mutual involvement in setting rules depends upon the careful cultivation of fairness and trust in the new family. This has to be learned by doing. The children have to experience fairness before trust can develop. Trust is not a verbalism; it is an experienced relationship. The family is always the primary learning place for trust or for distrust.

The relationship of the children to their natural parents should be the subject of open discussion. The child should never be made to feel that the loyalty to the other parent in any way threatens the well-being of the parents in the newly constructed family. Where there has been death, the memory of the deceased parent—or in the case of divorce, the visits to the parent—should be anticipated, planned for, and discussed in a natural manner. These ties are a vital part of the children's lives.

The remarriage that works includes a sensitive, understanding appreciation of the place of the children in the family and a respect for the feelings of the children, while at the same time resting upon a firm ground of fairness and love for each one.

Avoiding Failure

Remarriages need not fail, even though a large percentage of them have failed in the past few years. Look at the following list of frequently appearing stumbling blocks to successful remarriage, and ask yourself if these cannot be avoided:

1. Entry into marriage for the wrong reasons, i.e.,
   —to restore a damaged self-image
   —to find financial security
   —to provide a parent for children
   —to legalize a sexual relationship
2. Unresolved emotional baggage from a former marriage
3. Alcoholism (or other forms of escapism) on the part of one or both partners
4. Different values and goals
5. Lack of commitment to the marriage, or infidelity
6. Inability to communicate with each other
7. Misunderstandings about parenting children of former marriages or of the present one
8. Interference of family members (in-laws)
9. Cruelty or indignities

The startling fact about such a list is its similarity to the reasons why first marriages fail. Many people are shocked to find that they have failed the second time for the same reasons they failed in their first marriage. Until this resemblance is pointed out to them, these people may not even realize that they married a person remarkably similar to their first mate.

"How could I have repeated the same mistake?" is the question most often asked. "Can't I learn anything from my mistakes?" Of course a person *can*, but the issue is far more difficult than avoiding a mistake. The issue is whether either partner is willing to face the demands of a successful human relationship and to work to fulfill those demands.

The success of remarriages comes back to the application of the central principles of interpersonal dynamics:

—The balanced ledger of giving and receiving in life
—The reciprocal fairness implemented in the family
—The ability to be accountable and to hold others accountable
—The courage to contend for what is fair
—The courage to work through distorted relations

You are fortunate indeed if you have found someone with whom you are ready to share the years that lie ahead of you in love and trust and mutual care. This situation deserves your honesty and your integrity, the self that is truly you. Your remarriage can be strong and abiding, full of peace and joy.

106

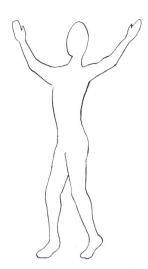

dimensions of a new life

There is evidence that we have entered an era of rediscovery of internal strength and mystic power. The rise of meditation groups, gurus, and charismatic leaders; the persistence and resurgence of religious groups; the popularity of astrology, esoteric movements, magic, and even witchcraft all point to the restless discontent with the limited resources of life normally thought to be all that are available. The search is for the source of power and for the source of being itself. For many, it means the first search for the redemptive power of God in their lives.

Single parents are among those who are learning that suffering and pain can open life to sources of psychic power which they didn't know existed. New life emerges from the crucible of pain. This insight is as old as childbirth and as compelling as the cross of the Christian church. When the conditions of life become unbearable, something has to happen; and when there is a reaching out for help, people find the upward spiraling of power available to those who can respond to it.

Suffering and pain call for change; and when sufficient power is called upon to make the changes, a new dimension of life comes forth. John Pfeiffer in his comprehensive work, *The Emergence of Man,* referred to this phenomenon as a mark that distinguishes the human species from what he labels the "stand patters" species of animals:

> Like other species, [man] is capable of adapting to change, but, even more significant, he no longer waits for change to occur. Instead of resisting or minimizing change and accepting it grudgingly, he goes out

and deliberately creates it, thereby creating new conditions to which he must adapt in new ways.[1]

People, at their mysterious center, have a persistent restlessness, a drive, a "kind of permanent and deliberate instability" that becomes a force in the area of their discontent and plunges them into "the search for novelty, exploration and missions. . . ."[2] The very forces that heighten consciousness and self-understanding point to the forces of the natural order that produce and sustain the life of the human family. Despite the subjectivity of most individual and general history, the world of psychic strength is the relatively uncharted world of discovery for the decades ahead.

Examine your track record as a single parent. It hasn't been easy, and you will never fully escape the stabbing pain and the return of suffering. But look at yourself—you have survived to this point. Around you you have seen others who have said, "I can't do it. I simply can't do it," and yet they do; they do survive. In the process you and they have called upon reserve strength you didn't know was available, and you have found the life force itself sustained by unseen conduits of life energy.

People in circumstances similar to your own have felt that they would have remained slaves to uncontrolled events, imprisoned by the actions of others, helpless to extricate themselves, had it not been for the realization that in the process of coping they were drawing on forces outside themselves—greater than their own—as well as forces within themselves which they didn't know they had. This awareness has put them on the track of something that has led to a lifting of their lives to a new level analogous to the creative leaps typical of the evolutionary emergence of humankind.

> Since "marriage and motherhood" was my most important goal in life, the realization that I had made a mistake was very painful. I had invested eleven years with a man I once loved very dearly. Our second child was still an infant when I began to feel the unhappiness in my heart.

> When I would try to discuss our problems with my husband and, at different times, the possibility of divorce, he would deliberately involve our first grade child as a pawn to keep me from leaving.

> The decision took six years. In my prayers that night I pleaded

[1] John Pfeiffer, *The Emergence of Man* (New York: Harper and Row, Publishers, 1969), p. 14.
[2] *Ibid.,* p. 435.

108

with God for guidance. The next morning I was dressed for housecleaning. It was a relatively small incident that "broke the camel's back." I stewed in my juice while I made the beds. When my husband left the house for an errand, I calmly took out the suitcases and packed as quickly as possible. It was as though a greater force was leading me with every deliberate movement.

The persistence of life itself is mystifying. Many people have expressed amazement when they have looked back on the record they have accumulated for improvising under pressure, coping against impossible demands, and surviving despite formidable odds. We often hear, "I didn't think I could do it, but I did." This coping capacity, this experience of survival often puts people on the track of the potential they have in themselves and the potential of the universe in which they live. However accustomed they may have been to putting themselves down, the fact remains that they have utilized surprising strength in order to survive and have grown tremendously in the process.

This level of self-awareness and self-congratulation is important in working through the aftermath of broken relationships. It is at this point of self-awareness that many people become conscious for the first time that, in order to survive and to cope, they have drawn upon psychic power beyond themselves that they hadn't known existed.

Prolonged periods of self-pity and oversympathetic shielding by family and friends may thwart the emergence of these psychic forces. There is a time for sympathy; there is a need for mourning in the aftermath of a broken relationship. You will never be completely free of that kind of mourning; but the time must come when one must begin to push against those emotions and to contend with the pressures of life, if healing is to be completed.

The knowledge of what you have done to date is a knowledge that can take you to the sources of your life and the sustaining power to live with a sense of dignity and a respect for the fullness of life. As May Sarton put it long ago in a poem entitled "Santos: New Mexico,"

> Return to the deep sources, nothing less
> Will nourish the torn spirit, the bewildered heart,
> The angry mind: and from the ultimate duress,
> Pierced with the breath of anguish, speak for love.[3]

At the source of your life there are signs of that flow of creative and sustaining power that enables life to persist on the planet. As you

---

[3] Quoted in Halford E. Luccock and Frances Brentano, eds., *The Questing Spirit* (New York; Coward, McCann & Geoghegan, Inc., 1947), p. 38. Copyright © 1942 by The Atlantic Monthly Company, Boston, Mass. Reprinted with permission.

see it at the roots of your own life, you may call it survival power, the will to live, or use the vocabulary of religion that is familiar to you; but explore and think about the power to live that emerges from the roots of your life. Henri Bergson called this the vital impulse *(l'elan vital)*—the core of reality which sustains life; provides continuity to one's own consciousness of being; and also supports one's advance on the road of time, gnawing into the future and swelling as it advances.

The more you bring to consciousness the powers you have drawn upon during a time of stress, the closer you will come to the release of power that the mystics desire, which the meditation disciples seek, and for want of which humanity is impoverished and deprived. Many hurting people today are discovering that the release of power in basic human relations can be found at the root of their own existence in the primary family.

An impressive record has been made by those who simply refused to engage in a way of life that, from their viewpoint, could hold no promise or satisfaction, even if it were successfully lived out according to the rules of that life. In the broadest sense, this fretful discontent and the risk-it-all search for the undiscovered stand behind most of the creative leaps in the history of human culture. It certainly is characteristic of persons who achieve a sense of dignity and respect for the fullness of their own lives in relationship to others.

110

The form of rebellion in the sixties and seventies has ranged from shocking self-destruction to mind-boggling idealism and achievement. Through it all, in quest of an unnamed freedom and self-realization, adolescents at ages fourteen, fifteen, and sixteen defy all the mores of the community; stand defiantly against their parents; and walk away from parental love, security, education, and everything that has been known. Their ability to do so is beyond comprehension. An observer on Telegraph Avenue in Berkeley, California, can see the throngs of adolescents who have split from the respectable ways of their parents in the East. The scene is the flip side of the record of pleading, threatening, reasoning, and storming which produced the adolescents' defiant "I'm goin'!"

This splitting from the familial roots is not offered as a model to anyone; but the untapped power which human beings have is revealed in the human resources which are required for an adolescent to stand alone against what has to be seen as hostile reaction to his or her intent. Someday the reckoning has to come, and the search for rootage will have to take place. A harnessing of psychic power in the individual combined with a grounding and support of that power in the sources of life itself can result in a newer, stronger humanity. Many who have faced staggering disruption in the pattern of their lives are ready to tap that same kind of exultant, vibrant power and bring it to bear on the quality of their lives and on the lives of other members of their primary and extended families.

The discontented youth have argued well that it is neither wise nor ethical to adjust one's own life to a life of discontent when deeper resources of life are available. This kind of talk may seem simplistic and unrealistic, and the methods of such youth for achieving their goals may be unacceptable to some; yet it rings a faint bell, especially for those parents who have had religious background and experience. The major religions have always proposed that human beings cannot handle well the deep issues of life and certainly can never adjust to the ultimate issues without resources from beyond the self.

People who have outgrown the religion of their childhood and have adopted the practical philosophies of life without reference to God, moral judgment, or any ultimate accountability, nonetheless often feel the promptings that all is not completely said and the case is not closed. Paul Engle summed it up for his generation:

> You say you buried God (weeping you say it)
> And split the flesh to its essential parts,
> But you have left us bodies bright with flame
> And buried God no deeper than our hearts.[4]

This age is programmed for producing turned-off people. We have learned how to rationalize the sense of divinity down into the inert form of innocuous doctrine and how to separate the religious performance from the base of power. This frees us to conduct our lives with accountability only to the self. We seem to operate conveniently according to the rules of our family of origin and our present and extended families until relational distortions strip these rules of meaning and support for us. Then comes that state of emptiness expressed in the anguished cry, "I can't go on." From this point, the distressed individual may begin to reconstruct a life without the mistakes of the past, using whatever new skills are needed but operating essentially within the same framework of self-understanding and life understanding. The tendency is to stay within safe boundaries, risking little in fear of repeating painful errors.

111

The alternative is to examine the evidence of what you are capable of doing and to root the future securely in the source of your being.

"Why was I brought to this hour?" One answer which has to be considered is: "Because otherwise you never would have known that there is something better." Contented and experiencing predictable

[4] *Ibid.*, p. 40.

support, a person is not apt to be seeking a fuller, more complete life. The pain and the suffering, while not sought either as ends or means, are well worth it if a new kind of rootedness in the source of life itself can emerge. If your experience in coping has taught you that you have reserves of psychic power and are supported by a relationship to a basic life force in the world, there would appear to be little advantage in standing still and dealing with the same round of existence.

What is proposed is something more than merely standing erect after going through the degradation of broken self-image and shattered relations. The tragic events of life can be utilized as key times of self-awareness which, with the resources you have identified, can carry you far beyond the practical levels of simply coping.

Whether or not you choose to risk exploring the unexplored, one thing is clear: It is impossible as a single parent for you to drop back and try to reconstruct the past patterns of life. It cannot be done, and it is a mistake to devote time and energy in attempting to do it. For example, it is a dead-end street to attempt to reproduce single-handedly that which formerly was the task of two adults. The ground rules have now changed. Even the introduction of a new partner to fill the void will not carry one back to what existed before. That act, too, carries a thrust toward a new pattern of life. It is not the absence of someone filling a role in the family that distresses you; it is the absence of a person, no matter how unpleasant the memory. The coming of a different person can only set up a new structure of relationships, requiring new kinds of adjustments.

112

The question, "How can I alone do what two of us were doing before?" cannot be allowed to close off hope. Forces beyond yourself are already at work and have thrust you into a new life plan whether you want it or not, and whether you choose to go it alone or seek help from another person or persons. It is impossible to reconstruct the past, and you tear yourself and your children apart attempting to do so. One woman said,

> It took me four years to realize I was grinding myself to pieces trying to keep the house painted, the lawns trimmed, the gardens growing—even the stamps collected and mounted just as my husband had done. I had to ask myself, "What am I doing?" Trying to prove to myself and the kids that it didn't happen? That he is still here?

Even if there is a conscious decision to sacrifice one's own life and the lives and future of the children in order to build a memorial to the one who is gone, the old ways of life simply cannot be restored. The separation has changed the relationships between you and the children, and you have to be able to speak from an "I" position, which will reflect with integrity your own ground.

Those who say, "I will hold things steady until I can marry again," are in error if they think that, by saying this, things will remain as they were or will fall back into place. Even the appropriate help of a brother, sister, mother, or father cannot hold things as they were. The uncompromising reality which becomes the ground of your own decision making is that the life pattern has been changed, something new is taking place, and something new is required of you.

At this point, will you choose merely to utilize your present skills and experiences as you enter this emerging future, or will you choose to regroup your skills and experience around values and self-concepts that have continuity with the past but also strain toward the future?

Men and women who have been brought up extolling the virtues of individualism, believing in self-reliance and privatized affairs, may find great inner anguish as they hear themselves saying, "I've had it; I need help from somewhere." As troubled and confused as the situation may be, it is not all bad that this struggle is going on. Actually, an injustice to yourself and to your children may be perpetuated if the commitment to self-reliance ("Leave me alone. I can manage.") is carried on out of habit, out of pride and loyalty to the past, or even because of present authority. The commitments that matter will be those that are made in connection with breaking through the present cycle of emptiness and despair.

113

Single parents who have had to struggle to stay afloat, to survive, may well be one of the key groups in American life to break open an exciting new dimension of life. Family therapists are saying that the American culture can no longer support and sustain either the individual or family life when the meanings of accountability, reciprocal justice, and intergenerational dynamics are so blatantly ignored or blindly attacked. They say that the hope for the restoration of society and the place where a new generation can learn the meaning of trust, fairness, and accountability must be in the primary family. If the child does not experience such values in his or her family of origin, it is unlikely that the child will ever learn how to trust or how to be just in other relationships. Deep within the adult lies the lessons learned in childhood about how trustworthy life and people are and what love and promises should mean.

At stake in the quest for the rootedness of life is not only the fulfilling life for yourself. Also at stake is the health of your future relationship and the lessons your children are learning about what music you dance to, what values control your being. The disruption of your life, however painful it is, may present a unique opportunity for enriching your heritage and the legacy you give to your children, provided you are willing to open your mind to new dimensions of feeling, hearing, seeing, even smelling and tasting; provided you are willing to risk and to invest in relationships with all those others with whom you come in contact; and provided you are willing to reach outside yourself for sources of strength that are within your grasp.

where to turn for help

Below is a sample listing of agencies which are available to help with specific problems:

Legal Aid Society or a lawyer's referral service is available in every major city and in many smaller ones. If not listed in the local telephone directory, call the local bar association.

Family Service, Inc., is listed in your local directory, provides counseling services for families, and is a good source of information about other mental health agencies.

Governor's Commission on the Status of Women is operable in nearly all states. Write to the State Office Building in your state capital.

For information about drugs or alcohol abuse, if there is no local agency, write or phone

National Clearinghouse for Drug Abuse Information
11400 Rockville Pike
Rockwall Building
Rockville, MD 20852   301/443-6500

National Clearinghouse for Alcohol Abuse Information
9119 Gaither Road
Gaithersburg, MD 20760   301/443-3860

Neighborhood Legal Services
Office of Legal Service
Office of Economic Opportunity
1200 19th Street N.W., Room 509
Washington, DC 20506

National Welfare Rights Organization
1420 N Street, N.W.
Washington, DC 20005

For other information about problems associated with the single parent life, write to
Reach Associates, Inc.
601 Burton Road
Oreland, PA 10975   215/233-1140

take me along

Measuring Things

Description: A math project for parent and child to increase observation, compare sizes and shapes, keep a careful record.

Age Level: 8-12

**Materials
Required:** Paper, pencil, ruler, yardstick, tape measure.

Procedure: Select one room of the house for this project. It might be the child's room or, if the parent has limited time, the kitchen or some other room where the parent will be doing other things part of the time.

If the child has been learning about the metric system, you may wish to record the measurements in both metric and decimal systems.

Make a list of everything you can see in the room— the tables, chairs, rug, lamps, books, doorways, etc. Draw lines on a piece of paper for columns.

Object	Height In.	Height Cm.	Width In.	Width Cm.	Depth In.	Depth Cm.
Table						
Chair						
Lamp						
Etc.						

Help the child get started. Maybe he or she can teach you about metric measurements.

Measure everything very carefully. Pretend you are engineers or carpenters who have to have very exact measurements.

When the list is finished, and all measurements recorded, decide what shapes things are. Was it possible to measure round or oval objects with the tools you have? How could you measure them?

Help the child find out about measuring things in other ways. Geometry is coming. He or she might get interested.

Most of all—have fun! Show somebody the record.

Nature Study

Description: A nature study project for parent and child to increase observation, learn the effects of nutrition, experiment in a scientific manner.

Age Level: 7-10

Materials Required: String, paper, pencil, small package of commercial fertilizer (10-5-5), water.

Procedure: Parent and child should select an area of grass in the yard. Mark off two squares side by side of three feet each. Examine minutely and record everything you can see in each of the squares. Make a map; mark on the map a number for each square. (Be sure that both squares will get the same amount of sunlight.)

Carefully remove any weeds from both squares, recording the number of such plants removed.

With an old fork or other sharp instrument, aerate the soil (punch holes over the whole surface) of square # 1. Then evenly distribute over the same square the amount of commercial fertilizer the package directions recommend. Water thoroughly, making sure not to water square #2, on a regular schedule.

If there is no rain for several days, you will want to continue to water square # 1 on a regular schedule.

Record weekly the changes in color, growth, etc. If you have a camera available, you may want to take some before and after pictures, or pictures at set intervals. Measure the grass. Draw some pictures.

At the end of one month, help the child write a report about what has been observed.

You may want to read some books about grass before starting the project. The library or a lawn supply store can help you find materials which are appropriate for your child's reading.

Help the child understand what he or she has seen. What conclusions might be drawn about nutrition for living things? He or she might consider the meaning for human growth, for himself or herself.

Most of all—have fun!

Field Trip with a Parent

Description: A study of how things grow and affect each other in the out-of-doors.

Materials
Required: Time

The Web of Life   119

Light, air, water, and soil are the elements of life,
Life is divided into producers, consumers, and decomposers.
Everything is becoming something else;
Everything has a home,
Homes in a defined area form a community,
Inhabitants of these communities live together in competition, cooperation, or neutrality;
Man is the chief predator.[1]

Procedure: Take your child for a walk. Walk slowly. See how many kinds of houses you can find—houses for people, for insects, for animals.

What kinds of communities can you find?

[1] Steve Van Matre, *Acclimatization* (Martinsville, Ind.: American Camping Association, 1972), p. 5. Reprinted with the permission of the American Camping Association.

What is being produced?

What is being consumed?

What is decomposing?

What inhabitants are competing? Cooperating? Being neutral?

What have people done to disturb this action?

Try this same walk at another time of year—is it different in winter, for example?

Most of all—have fun!

Exploring the Family Heritage

Description: Helping children understand who they are through a look at the generations before them.

Age level: 10 and older

Materials Required: Family records, family photos

120

You will want to enlist the help of other members of your extended family who have records, photographs, diaries, letters, or other memorabilia which could be useful to you.

This can be a short-term or long-term project, depending on the interest you and/or your children have in it. Introduce the idea as if it were to be a short-term idea; then if they get excited about it, propose that you look further into the possibilities of composing a more complete family history.

Begin with the usual kind of family tree, such as that shown below. Fill in the squares and circles (square for male, circle for female). You may wish to make it more complete by adding details such as the marriages of the various persons and the children they have produced, etc.

This particular diagram shows only one side of the family. The children may want to do the same thing for the other parent.

Collect anecdotes as you work on your family's history, perhaps encouraging the children to interview older members of the family. They and the children will enjoy sharing memories of their childhood.

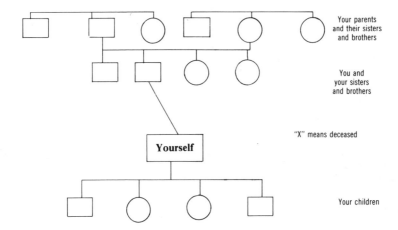

Your parents
and their sisters
and brothers

You and
your sisters
and brothers

"X" means deceased

Yourself

Your children

121

how to write successful résumés

When you apply for a job, the résumé you submit may be the "make or break" factor in your getting the position. Personnel departments receive so many applications for jobs that they must find a way to weed out some of the applicants. Very often, this is done by selecting those persons who have prepared a résumé which is easy to read, makes a good appearance, and provides the necessary information. There are many clues in the résumé as to the kind of employee you would be. For example, a personnel director might ask:

Does the applicant care enough about finding a job to prepare the résumé carefully?

Is he or she an orderly person, who can express himself or herself well?

Does he or she tell me enough about the kinds of experience he or she has had for me to determine his or her qualifications for the job?

These reasons alone are enough to make you want to present a positive impression. In addition, having a well-prepared résumé ready to mail if you hear of an opening will save you lots of time when you are submitting applications to a number of possible employers.

Study the enclosed sample. Then rough out a résumé for yourself. Check it for accuracy yourself, and have someone else read it over to see if all of the necessary information has been included. Note the following items on the attached sample (they are number-keyed to the sample).

1. Your name should appear in bolder type than the rest of the résumé. Include your address and telephone number.

2. Personal History. You may or may not want to include all of the items shown here. It is not required for you to show your marital status or the name of a spouse; but if you do, this is the place for it.

3. Education. Include here all of your formal education. List high school graduation, high school equivalency, or highest level in the high school. (If you did not graduate from high school, it will pay

for you to take a high school equivalency exam, usually available in an adult evening school.) Higher education should include degrees received and your major. Include also any continuing education, such as seminars or training courses.

4. Employment Record. Beginning with your most recent employment, and, arranged according to dates, describe the kinds of work and responsibilities you have had in some detail. The title of the position really doesn't explain the job, and a prospective employer will want to know more of the details. For example, if your experience was in the computer field, you might say,

> *Business Information Systems:* developed and implemented accounting, marketing, order processing, and inventory control systems for clients in a wide variety of industries, such as wholesaling and distribution, mail order, retail, manufacturing and assembly, and labor unions.

If you have had experience driving heavy equipment, doing machine tooling, or handling receptionist-secretarial work, describe the types of responsibilities and equipment.

If you held several positions for one company, you will want to detail the kinds of responsibilities you had in each position, in chronological order, which will show your progression within the company.

124

You may wish to separate the various fields of experience you have had, listing positions held in each field. The border headings then might be "Consulting Experience," "Academic Experience," etc.

5. Military Experience. Some employers like to know if you have served in the armed forces. If you have, include it here; but if not, eliminate the item. You would not, for example, deliberately call attention to the fact that you did not serve in the armed forces by listing Military Experience and then writing "None."

6. Community Activities. Your future employer can tell a good deal about the kind of person you are by the volunteer activities in which you participate. Most companies like to have their employees involved in community activities; so list them, showing positions of leadership you have held. Include such things as Scout committee, volunteer fire department, school board member, etc.

7. References. Many people prefer to say, "References furnished upon request." Others include them. If you do, check with the persons you are listing to be certain they know that you are

including their names, and ask for their permission to do so. In this way, if an inquiry is received from the prospective employer, they will not be surprised.

References should not be relatives. They should be persons who have some knowledge of the kind of experience you have had and your ability to perform. You may wish to include one person as a character reference, but employers prefer the names of people who can discuss your fitness for the job.

8. You may wish to include a request that the prospective employer not contact your present employer without your knowledge. If so, at the bottom of each sheet, type in bold print: PLEASE DO NOT CONTACT MY PRESENT EMPLOYER WITHOUT MY PRIOR KNOWLEDGE.

Résumés should be submitted in person, even if only to the receptionist in a personnel office. Sometimes, however, a newspaper advertisement will specify that the résumé should be submitted by mail. If so, send it with a brief cover letter, such as:

Gentlemen:

The résumé I am enclosing is a brief summary of my professional and academic experience. I would welcome the opportunity to discuss it with you in more detail.

Thank you for your consideration.

Sincerely,

(sign here in ink)

(your name typed here)

Enclosure

125

JAMES A. JACKSON
143 Nittany Lane
Meriden, CT 06450
203/433-2165

(2) Personal History	Date of Birth: 7/23/34 (5) Military: U.S. Army
	Marital Status: Divorced Quartermaster
	Children: 3

(3) Education	Springfield H.S., Springfield, Mass.
	Colgate University (2 years)
	Human Relations, Management seminars
(4) Employment Record	
1969– Present	*Lexon Publishing Company* Meriden, Connecticut Manager, Periodical Distribution Department
	Recruitment, supervision, development, and appraisal of personnel; preparation and administration of budget; purchase of supplies, equipment, and services; order processing, customer relations; maintenance of customer mailing lists.
1958-1969	*S. S. Kresge Company* Detroit, Michigan
	Management training in stores in 5 cities in the northeast. Managed stores in Providence, Rhode Island; Washington, D.C.; and Philadelphia, Pennsylvania. Complete responsibility for hiring, firing, and training of up to 50 employees. Buying of merchandise; inventory and stock control, including annual inventory.
1956–1958	Armed Services
(6) Community Activities	American Red Cross—Bloodmobile Treasurer, Friends of the Library, 1973–1975 Co-President, Secondary PTA Board of Deacons, Valley Baptist Church
(7) References	Furnished on request
	(8) PLEASE DO NOT CONTACT MY PRESENT EMPLOYER WITHOUT MY PRIOR KNOWLEDGE.

126

(1) SALLY J. HOPE
22 Laguna Ave.
San Diego, CA 92123

(2) Personal History	Date of Birth: 2/15/51 Marital Status: Widowed Children: 2
(3) Education	Bayshore H.S., San Diego, Calif. San Diego Jr. College (1 year) Commercial Business Center, Typing
(4) Employment Record	
1975–Present	*Oceanside Medical Center* Typist and Filing Clerk
1968–1970	*Overseas Shipping, Inc.* Filing Clerk
(6) Community Activities	Girl Scouts, Den Mother Friends of the Library Red Cross Fund Solicitation
(7) References	Furnished on request
	(8) PLEASE DO NOT CONTACT MY PRESENT EMPLOYER WITHOUT MY PRIOR KNOWLEDGE.

putting the pieces together

Help For Single Parents

Leader's Guide
by Velma Thorne Carter
and J. Lynn Leavenworth

contents

introduction

The authors have been working for several years with families who have experienced broken relationships and are struggling with the transition to a new life-style. In groups ranging from ten to twenty persons, individuals come to understand what is happening to them, to connect with resources available to them, and then to turn from despair to hope, and from hope to growth toward an intentional life-style for them and their children.

The group setting for these educational experiences has provided support for the individuals as they gain strength from the progress and encouragement of others. This is not "group therapy" per se, although the hundreds of men and women who have participated in the groups attest to the therapeutic aspects of the experience. Nor is the purpose of the group merely to provide some empathic "stroking" with assurance that everything will be all right. Recovery from the trauma of separation, divorce, or death is painful, and persons going through these broken relationships need to have their pain acknowledged and be encouraged to face some of the hard issues that are involved. Facing these realities is an important step on the road back from despair.

131

Synagogues and churches have found this involvement with single parents to be a valid extension of the healing ministry to a hurting segment of the population. One Methodist minister told us, "Working with single parents has opened new dimensions in my ministry and in my understanding of the Christian gospel."

This *Leader's Guide* is a tool for conducting a study group or seminar for single parents on the themes of the book. The materials are prepared for use with custodial and noncustodial parents, and the groups should include both men and women if possible, in order to give a balance to the discussion.

The objectives for the study groups are to provide single parents with help in:

—Facing the pain of broken relationships

—Identifying available resources

—Relinquishing the past

—Parenting responsibly

—Learning from the past

—Relating values to life goals

—Building creative relationships

—Preparing for remarriage

—Connecting with hitherto unknown strength

The Need for Study Groups

A growing percentage of the population needs help in working through the distorted feelings that lie in the wake of separation, divorce, and widowhood. The failure of the basic social institutions of the community to provide the kinds of help needed as well as the lack of preventive services, has led to tragic suffering and personal dysfunction, often at great financial cost to the community. Consider these statistics:

—There were 1,026,000 divorces in the United States last year (1975), compared with 2,126,000 marriages.[1]

—There are more than one million widows with at least one child in their care.[2]

—There are about 1,500,000 legal separations annually in the United States.[3]

—"Over seven million children under eighteen years of age are living with their mothers and without their fathers."[4]

During the first few months following the disruption of a marriage, men and women find themselves subject to conflicting emotions and a bewildering array of practical and personal problems. Often confused and frustrated, they know they need help but do not

[1] "The number of marriages was lower in 1975 than in any year since 1968. The number of divorces has increased every year since 1962 and has more than doubled from 1966 to 1975." *Monthly Vital Statistics Report,* Public Health Service (Rockville, Maryland: U.S. Department of Health, Education & Welfare), vol. 24, no. 13, p. 12.

[2] Jane K. Burgess, "The Single-Parent Family: A Social and Sociological Problem," *The Family Coordinator* (April, 1970), pp. 137-144.

[3] *Ibid.*

[4] Elizabeth Herzog and Cecelia E. Sudia, "Families Without Fathers," *Childhood Education,* vol. 48, no. 4 (January, 1972), pp. 175-181.

know where to turn. Though some communities offer excellent mental health services, the single parent may be one of the many who still feel that only "sick" people go there. The educational experience offered in the study group may be seen as the first evidence that the community understands and cares about their needs.

Sponsorship of the Study Groups

The type of study group experience projected in this guide may be sponsored by community institutions and agencies, such as religious groups (a church, synagogue, or a group of religious institutions), YMCAs, YWCAs, YMHAs, YWHAs, adult evening schools, PTAs, libraries, singles' groups, schools, colleges, business corporations, and mental health agencies.

When an organization sponsors a study group, it means that it gives the project endorsement, encourages attendance, actively promotes the group, provides scholarships (optional), or may subsidize it. Expenses for competent and trained leaders and other costs are usually paid for out of fees charged to the participants. Except in rare instances, all participants should pay all or some part of the fee.

Promotion of Study Groups

A theme title, such as "Getting It All Together," and a descriptive phrase indicating an educational seminar for single parents should be used in all promotional material. 133

Newspaper write-ups with pictures of leaders, the statement of objectives, etc., are effective for recruitment. Radio and TV spot announcements may be used to reach those who are not among the constituency of the sponsoring group(s). Attractive flyers with a registration tear-off portion may be placed in churches, schools, libraries, etc. Some personal contact should be made with clergy, school guidance staffs, and mental health centers to enlist the support of these key people. Often these helping agents are willing to make a personal contact with someone they know who could benefit from such a program.

A maximum of twenty persons and a minimum of ten should be the goal for enrollment. More than twenty makes it difficult to hear individual concerns; less than ten prevents flexibility in small group discussions.

Setting for the Group

The size of the room is important. A single room is adequate, provided there is space enough for small group discussions, but the room should not be so large that the group will feel ill at ease—the church parlor or a large classroom would be ideal. We like to have participants seated around a table; eye contact is easier this way, and it is more difficult for anyone to become merely an "observer."

Equipment and Supplies

A companion book, *Putting the Pieces Together,* containing only the first 128 pages of this *Leader's Guide* is the basic resource for this series of sessions. It will be identified in the *Leader's Guide* as the Resource Book. Each participant should have a copy for personal use.

Besides tables, chairs, adequate lighting, and other basic equipment, the following will be needed:

Chalkboard, chalk and erasers, or newsprint and felt-tipped pens

Scratch pads and pencils

A manila folder for each person

A tape recorder (optional)

Posters, humorous or serious, cut-outs, or cartoons can be used to enliven the room. All worksheets illustrated in the session guides should be reproduced and ready before the seminar begins. (If books for individual participants are used, a sufficient number of copies of these worksheets may be reproduced without obtaining specific permission from the publisher.)

134

The Teaching Team

The sensitive nature of the discussions requires a skilled teaching team, persons who have had experience in counseling and in group techniques. You may be able to recruit a family counselor from one of the public agencies in your area, a pastor, or social worker. We prefer to use two people, one male, one female (not husband and wife). Ideally, one of the two should be a single parent who has been successful in getting himself or herself together after divorce or the death of a spouse. The leaders may wish to bring in other resource persons, such as an attorney, a child psychologist, a CPA, or a competent realtor, according to the needs of the group.

All of the persons on the teaching team must have thorough preparation for the task before the group begins. Part of the training must include a careful study of the goals, content, and method of each session. Getting to know one another will allow the team to work together with a feeling of trust. The openness and freedom of expression among the leaders give "permission" to the group to speak with candor, and from an "I" position. The sponsors of the group may wish to know the position held by team members on sensitive subjects, such as remarriage and abortion, and these matters should be discussed candidly before the sessions begin.

Curriculum

The material that follows assumes a series of eight sessions, and there is an alternate session which may be substituted for one of these. Some groups may wish to spend more than one session on a subject such as parenting. Leaders should gain an early commitment for the eight sessions, one night a week for two hours each. The experience of the group is cumulative, and it is important that members give priority to the group in planning schedules.

The study group can be the means by which persons facing anxiety, stress, and frustration can move toward an intentional lifestyle that is satisfying and fulfilling.

135

session 1
you are not alone

Projection

The objectives of this session are to help everyone feel comfortable in the group; to establish an agenda for the eight weeks; to hear the concerns of each participant; and to begin uncovering the resources that are available to the individual.

Preparation

Leaders should visit community agencies (mental health, family services, religious) in order to collect information about community resources that you will share with the group. Reproduce the chart "Dynamics of Single Parent Adjustment," so that you have on hand one copy for each participant. You will need registration blanks, name tags, newsprint and felt-tip markers or chalkboard and chalk, and coffee or other refreshments if desired.

Conducting the Session

1st Mod:*   Welcome the group, emphasizing that this is to be
Getting   an educational experience. Ask each person to
to Know   make a commitment to attend all eight sessions and
You   to be as open as the leaders in sharing their own
experience. Review the objectives for the group (see
the Introduction of the *Leader's Guide*).

Use any effective device you are comfortable with to help people
get to know each other. You might, for instance, use "2 x 2," which
means two people talk to each other for two minutes, share three
important facts about themselves, and when the group reassembles,
each introduces one's partner to the group with those three facts.

Distribute the chart "Dynamics of Single Parent Adjustment"
and explain it to the group. This chart represents in the outer circles
the kinds of issues that are of concern to most single parents. Each of
these impacts one's interpersonal relations, self-concept, and values.
As one begins to solve these and other problems, the three areas move
into closer congruence and can be seen as helping the individual to
put his or her life in order—getting it all together.

2nd Mod: In this part of the session, you want to find out
Identifying   something about the expectations of the group,
the Problems where individuals are hurting, what problems they
are facing, and the kinds of help they are seeking.

Let the group know the leaders are not asking more of the group
than they themselves are willing to do. Share with them some of the
pain of your own life, demonstrating the use of an "I" position; that is,
you might say, "I am divorced, and a noncustodial parent . . ."; or "I
was raised in a single parent home; my mother died . . ."; "I know
something about abandonment, since my father was an alcoholic."
Then ask each person in turn to speak to his or her situation and
needs.

During this time, you should listen closely for clues that will be
part of your agenda for later sessions, listing key words or phrases on
the chalkboard:

Loneliness	Abandonment	Guilt
Care of children	Legalities	Custody of children
Sexual needs	Child support	Relationships with former spouse

*"Mod" is short for "module" and is used to indicate a sequence of development;
in some cases you may wish to alter the sequence, putting 2nd Mod before 3rd Mod,
etc., in some of the sessions.

You may wish to alter the order or content of the sessions, based on the needs of the group.

3rd Mod: Refer to the first chapter of the Resource Book, p.
Finding 15, which uses the paradigm of birth to illustrate
Resources how humans survive the trauma of change. Use this same process with the group.

Distribute any resource materials you have collected from the various agencies in your area, and explain them as fully as you can.

Resources which are available to individuals fall into several categories:

Personal	Fraternal
Familial	Financial
Community	Spiritual

Each of these is discussed fully in chapter 1 of the Resource Book.

Before closing the session, ask if there is any problem of urgent concern that needs to be discussed.

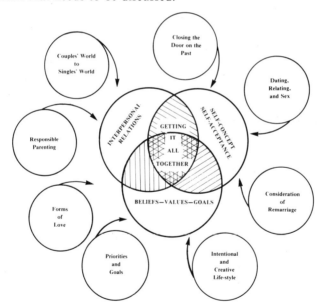

137

GETTING IT ALL TOGETHER: DYNAMICS OF SINGLE PARENT ADJUSTMENT©

© Reach Associates, Inc.

session 2
closing the door

Reflection

In an atmosphere of trust and candor set by the first session, and speaking from the "I" position of personal experience, the group in this session is ready to deal with personal and emotional ties that may block the future.

Projection

The objective is to encourage individuals to face their dependencies on the past and to become freed to move ahead. This session provides group support for individuals to examine their own "stuck" relationships, especially with members of the primary family, and to rework relationships that are still viable.

Preparation

Prepare for subgroup discussions (3 persons each); have chalkboard or newsprint available. Duplicate the chart of "Stages of Adjustment" from chapter 6 of the Resource Book unless members will have copies of the book with them.

Conducting the Session

1st Mod:
Raising
the
Issues
After introducing the subject of "closing doors" based on chapter 2 of the Resource Book, review the basic issues by asking the group to analyze what it means to "close the doors" in the case of Anne, Jack, and the person quoted on page 32. Using the buzz session technique, let groups of two or three persons turn toward each other to discuss these examples and to list the emotional ties to the past that can hinder personal development. After ten minutes ask the groups to report the most important issues for chalkboard listing. When all have reported, the leaders should attempt to sort out the key issues. Discussion may be limited to clarifying the statements.

2nd Mod:
Emotional
Adjustments
Be sure that the group has copies of "Stages of Adjustment" found in chapter 6 of the Resource Book. If members of the seminar do not have individual copies of the Resource Book with them, you may hand out duplicated copies. In a plenary session discuss the phases for clarification. Encourage discussion by asking: "From your experience, how would you change the sequences of adjustment?"

Drawing upon material in chapter 2 of the Resource Book, discuss the natural role of the mourning process and the need to bring it to a close.

Again drawing upon chapter 2, involve the group in a discussion of the reasons for guilt and the need to confront the persons involved. Illustrate the dangers that follow when guilt is buried under frenetic activities.

3rd Mod:
Loneli-
ness
In introducing the topic of loneliness, distinguish between "being alone" and "loneliness." The presence of grief or guilt often turns potentially creative experiences of being alone into enervating experiences of loneliness. The central issue is that *everyone* is lonely at times; the real question is, "What are you willing to do about it?"

Ask the group to list the times and circumstances when loneliness is felt the most, such as: "in the middle of the night," "holidays," etc. Write these replies on the chalkboard or newsprint and place them in general categories. Divide the group into subunits of three persons each; assign one of the above categories to each; instruct the subgroups to discuss how to overcome those difficult experiences of loneliness. Drawing upon their own experiences and the experience of others, each group is asked to list the ways in which people cope with the particular form of loneliness.

Ask the subgroups to report their findings to the total group; ask for further suggestions from the others following each report.

139

session 3
you and your love

Reflection

Consideration of grief, guilt, and loneliness suggest patterns of human interaction that condition what is given and received in intimate human relations. The review of persistent and sometimes debilitating emotions can be carried another step by looking at the love relationship.

Projection

After describing five forms of love expectation, the purpose is to enable each individual to relate what is given and received in love to needs that grow out of the person's distinctive heritage. Neither the described forms nor the questionnaire is authoritative even though they are developed from clinical experience. They provide interesting ways to enable the group to see reasons for possible incompatibility between people and the reasons for working to make the relationship better.

Preparation

Be sure that participants will have copies of "Graph Your Own Style of Loving" found in chapter 3 of the Resource Book. Arrange tables for writing.

Conducting the Session

1st Mod:
Who Am "I"?

Demonstrate on chalkboard the different ways in which the "I" can be perceived in a simple statement, "I love you."

The "I" as I see myself	The "I" that others see
The "I" which I would like to be	The "I" that my actions reveal.

When these distinctions are understood, show how they affect the articulation of the love relationship.

2nd Mod: Briefly describe the five forms of love referred to in
Forms of   chapter 3 of the Resource Book. The material is
Love   adapted by permission of *Psychology Today* from
an article that appeared October, 1974. The five
terms may be placed at the points of intersecting
triangles as follows:

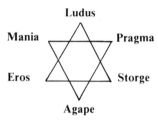

"Agape" is added to complete the triangles but represents a love that
asks nothing of the beloved and is rarely found in the clinic. It is a
pure, self-giving love.

The points of the star do represent tension points in human
relations. Thus Mania and Pragma are in tension in what is expected
of love; it is likely that they can meet each other's needs only if they
both work at their relationship.

Emphasize that no individual fits neatly into these forms, but
they are useful for self-understanding and to open discussion.   141

3rd Mod: Use the form "Graph Your Own Style of Loving" in
Charting   chapter 3 of the Resource Book and explain the
Your   marking system. *Study this marking system* in
Own   advance so you can give clear, consistent
Love   instruction. Explain that this is not a personality or
a psychological inventory, but a popular form drawn from clinical
experience to stimulate self-awareness and critical discussion.

Ask each person to fill out the form and tabulate the results.
Emphasize that there are no "right" or "wrong" answers and that the
reasons for marking a given question are as suggestive as the overall
tabulation. For example, take any one of the questions and
encourage the group to consider what the difference would be if it
were answered with "Almost Never" or "Almost Always."

In explaining the use of the form, make it clear that if the
person's answer is "Almost Always," she or he should circle *all* of the
AA's that appear on that line, or if it is "rarely true," then all of the R's
should be circled.

To tabulate, ask each person to add the number of circled answers in each vertical column. These totals should be combined for the 35 items to find the score for "Eros," "Ludus," etc. No item should be left blank, but the closest answer should be chosen if the user is uncertain. Emphasize that this "test" is only a discussion starter and is not a scientific measuring instrument.

After the tabulation and the discussion for clarification (usually there is much good-natured, spontaneous sharing of the results), encourage the members to compare the results with the way they perceive themselves. Also ask individuals to relate what it means to them that they answered a given question in one way instead of another. Would each of them, for example, be a different kind of person if, in truth, he or she would have had to choose a different answer?

session 4
responsible parenting

142

Reflection

Your efforts thus far in the sessions have been directed toward helping those in the group to face some of the "unfinished business" in their lives. Responsible parenting may be seen as both a burden and a source of great joy, but it is never finished, and all parents need to review their skills from time to time in an effort to do a better job of relating to their children.

Projection

The purpose in this session will be to help individuals in your group to understand that their children have the same kinds of emotional needs they themselves have, to increase their courage to parent responsibly, and in some measure to increase parenting skills.

Preparation

Read chapter 4 in the Resource Book. If possible, have on hand for sale or loan some of the books recommended in the bibliography. It may help the leaders to reflect on the quality of parenting they received from their own parents, and how it has affected their relationship to their children.

Make copies of the paragraph written by Dr. Barbara Krasner included with this session material to distribute to the group (or use some other piece you find appropriate).

You may wish to make a poster-size copy of the chart on p. 64 of the Resource Book.

Conducting the Session

1st Mod: **Raising** **Issues**	Begin the session with an explanation of the rights of children (see the chapter on Responsible Parenting in the Resource Book). Ask the group to react to your list (to which you may have added some other items), and if they wish, allow them to add others.

Make certain that you are thoroughly conversant with each of these points, so that you will be able to deal with the issues. You are most apt to get an argument from the group on the matter of contact with the noncustodial parent and on matters of accountability. You may wish to include a discussion of the chart on page 64 of the Resource Book.

Draw a large circle on the chalkboard and ask each person (including leaders) to place his or her name on the circle. Then extend a line outward on which the names of each of that person's children are to be written. Note ages under the names.

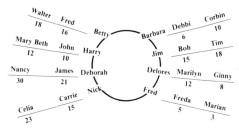

143

While at the board, ask each person to identify any child or children whose adjustment is a concern to the parent, and have them specify what the concern is.

You might want to have someone count the number of children in each age group: preschool, 6—12, teenage, and those over 21.

2nd Mod: **Perspective**	Divide the group into subgroups of three or four and ask individuals to discuss with one another their own experience of being parented. Who did the disciplining? Was each child in the family treated fairly? Did parents give of themselves to you? Was

communication good? Are you carrying any grudges against parents for injustices? These kinds of questions may help to open the discussion of what one received from parents, and what the relationship between group members and their parents now is.

3rd Mod: When the group reassembles, ask one of the persons
Facing who identified a difficult problem with a child to get
Issues in the "Hotseat." That simply means that you will deal specifically with the problems of that person's child. Ask for a more detailed explanation of the problem, a description of the child generally, and then ask that your subject try to relate his or her relationship with the child to the individual's experience of being parented (Mod 2). How do the two experiences seem to be parallel or different? The group and the

---

144

Every man and every woman is entitled to pursue the privilege of a fulfilled and a fruitful existence. They are also obliged to help their children grow into responsible human beings who in turn can bring the power of their lives to bear on the lives of their parents. Every woman and every man is entitled to pursue pleasure and avoid pain. They are also obliged to face the pain in life that is inevitable and even life-producing. They are obliged to face the pain that is generated by the structure of existence itself. That is, at the very least they are obliged to face and to act on the pain that is involved in responsible parenting and in appropriate filial concern and reciprocity. No-fault divorce can never lead to a no-fault clause in the parent-child relationship. Parental availability and accountability are conditions that accompany birth. They are conditions that can limit and circumscribe the peripheries of life when children are very young. Parental availability and accountability are also conditions that can deepen and broaden the meaning and the quality of life. Properly invested and employed, they can constitute a model for relatedness that may yet change the face of the earth. Girls and boys conceived in love, experiencing justice, learning compassion, developing loyalty to family members who relate dialogically, and reciprocating what they have received are the promise and the hope of every liberation movement. They are the stuff with which the world can be redeemed.

—Barbara R. Krasner*
1975

*from "Sublime Anthropomorphism": The Significance of Jewish Mysticism for Personal and Communal Existence (Unpublished Doctoral Dissertation, Temple University, 1975, Department of Religion). Dr. Krasner is a faculty member of the Department of Religion of Franklin and Marshall College; Relational Therapist, Human Systems Council, King of Prussia, Pennsylvania.

leaders should try to uncover resources that may be of assistance to the parent in the Hotseat, or some new approaches, but the leaders should make certain the answers are not in conflict with the principles established in Mod 1.

Put as many people successively in the Hotseat as time will permit. You may not have time to cover all of the more serious problems, and if so, you may want to eliminate one of the other sessions in order to continue at more depth on parenting.

Leave the group members with a positive note by reminding them that they cannot be both mother and father to their children, but they can be *parent*.

session 5
realistic goals

Reflection

The four previous sessions have been dealing with the past as "prologue to the future." By this time those who came to the group with feelings of despair should have begun to find strength in the group and a trust relationship within which they can open themselves to full participation as the group turns to planning for the future.

145

Projection

The leaders will help the group to understand the value of setting some realistic goals for themselves and their families. Setting obtainable goals and preparing a timetable for accomplishing them will be the purpose of the session. This will help to lay the groundwork for discussing self-fulfillment and remarriage later on.

Preparation

Read carefully chapter 5 of the Resource Book. Obtain from the Census Bureau the latest life-expectancy figures and make a copy for each person. Reproduce some form of the scale shown on page 73 in chapter 5. You might want to prepare a folder for retaining the goals agreed on by the individual, which might consist of cutting up a road map to an appropriate size and writing on the front with felt-tip marker: "Road Map to My Future."

Conducting the Session

1st Mod:
Raising
Issues

Begin with a discussion of the life-expectancy chart, asking each person to find his or her own age and noting how many years are remaining in his or her life expectancy. This helps to dramatize the need for life planning, since most of the group will see they have a lot of years yet to live. One of the leaders should graph his or her own life on the scale given in chapter 5 of the Resource Book, explaining the variations, the ups and downs illustrated. Ask each group member to do the same with his or her own chart.

2nd Mod:
Selecting
Destina-
tion

Divide the group into pairs, and if necessary put an extra person with one of the pairs. Ask each person to "dream"—to think creatively about what one would like to do in one's life. The partner should facilitate the process by asking questions that "push" for specifics, not allowing the dreamer to say simply "I want to be happy," but asking him or her to move on to "What would make you happy?"

As each person finishes his or her list of goals, he or she becomes the facilitator, helping the partner to do the same thing.

When both partners are finished, they may join another pair, and the four people will work at solving any problems or discussing roadblocks that are apparent to any member.

146

3rd Mod:
Unblock-
ing

Each group of four persons selects a leader who will keep the process moving. Each person in turn explains the goals she or he has selected, and the group will ask questions to determine whether goals are realistic. The group will also help in deciding on the first steps to be taken, difficulties that may be encountered, persons to be considered, arrangements to be made, and costs involved.

Most of the questions will have to do with long-term goals, and there may be some people in the group who are not ready to look at the long-range. They may have to consider some short-term goals, but the process is the same.

Impress on the group that the leaders are going to press hard to get each person to set up some kind of tentative timetable and to outline some specific steps he or she plans to take. Let the individuals take home the papers they have been working on to fill out details, but ask them to bring them back next session, and allow time for each person to arrange for a time to meet separately with one of the leaders to discuss his or her plans. Assign each person to one leader or another.

You may want to consider having a check-up time when leaders will contact group members, perhaps two or three months from the date of the meeting, in order that there be some feeling of accountability for carrying through.

session 6
fully alive in the singles' world

Reflection

After facing the needs for "uncoupling," for coping, and for developing a purposeful, intentional living style, the group is prepared to consider self-fulfillment and satisfaction in the singles' world.

Projection

This session will consider the motivations for stepping into the singles' world; discuss factors in dating again, experiences in forming new adult relationships with both sexes, and handling sexual needs.

Preparation

Obtain copies of the newsletters from the local singles' organizations (e.g., Parents Without Partners) for distribution. Provide chalkboard or newsprint for sessions. Recruit a panel of four single parents to relate their experiences of adjusting to the singles' world. In an advance session with the panel thoroughly prepare them to understand your objectives and approach.

Conducting the Session

1st Mod: **Raising** **Issues**	Brainstorm the group's understanding of the difference between the relationships in the couples' world and the singles' world. List the differences on the chalkboard. You may ask the group to call out differences experienced under the following categories:

Adult friends (when married; now as a single)
Types of organizations you participate in
Experiences in eating out
Relations with your extended family.
Relation to your children
Anxieties and fears
Habits and routines
Other:

2nd Mod: **Relational** **Perspective:** **Leader Input**	In forming new relationships, consider the principles for satisfactory long-term human relationships. To dramatize the give-and-take of relating to another, place a balance scale on the table as you review and discuss the following:

148

1. A balance of giving and receiving is required in satisfactory human relations. Imbalance occurs when a person feels that she or he is always giving without receiving or always receiving without an opportunity to give. Inability to give back produces guilt, and relationships are distorted.

2. It is difficult to give love or trust or personal support if it has not been received in one's legacy in the primary and extended family. Each of us comes into a relationship with a legacy from our family of origin.

3. Mutual accountability is fundamental to sound relationships. Partners have to hold each other accountable, letting it be known when needs are not being met. When weaknesses or neglect are covered up or excused, partners do each other an injustice that inevitably weakens the relationships.

(From time to time you may use the scale, adding weights to one side or the other to demonstrate imbalance of giving and receiving. Invite group members to give illustrations from their own experience and drawn upon your own marital experience to show how you or your partner has felt the "ledger" to be getting out of balance.)

These relationships usually can be applied in other basic

interpersonal actions, such as that between parent and child or between employer and employee. Basic fairness, a balance of giving and receiving, is as essential to labor relations as it is to marital relations.

3rd Mod: Introduce the panel, asking each to share his or her
Sharing marital status, the length of time being single, etc.
Experiences (The panel will be prepared to discuss the issues that have arisen in the first two mods as well as other issues they consider important.) A team member should chair the panel, keeping discussion on the topic and not allowing individual domination of the discussion. Other team members may draw out the panel for clarification or to cover neglected points. One member should be prepared to summarize the session.

Encourage discussion between the group and the panel. Follow the major themes until the closing time of the session.

Make necessary announcements or preparations for the next session.

149

alternate session
handling sexual needs

Projection

The purpose of this session is to connect value systems and healthy relational interaction to the practices of sexual intercourse. Every effort must be made to avoid being judgmental or giving conclusions to others. The individuals must be encouraged to review critically their own values and practices.

Preparation

Leaders should spend some time discussing their own values and the way in which their personal position on sexual behavior has evolved. If asked, it is appropriate for leaders to share with the group their position on sex, each leader speaking for himself or herself but, in doing so, they should be careful not to "wipe out" anyone who holds a different position.

Conducting the Session

1st Mod:
Clarifying
the Issues

Use the following or your own form of values clarification: Put on chalkboard a series of statements about sexual needs, identifying them with numbers, such as:

1. I would not engage in sexual intercourse outside of marriage under any circumstances.
2. I think it is OK to have sex with a partner with whom I am having a serious relationship.
3. I would not go very far into a relationship before finding whether my companion is a good sex partner.
4. I don't really know where I stand on sex.
5. I don't have any hangups about having sex with whomever I'm dating.

Assign each person to an area, which you have identified with the numbers above, thereby "defending" the statement so numbered.

Ask each group to spend ten or fifteen minutes together deciding what the rationale is for their position, and preparing to discuss that position with the total group.

When all are reassembled, hear the position of each group. Then ask if any would like to change their position and join one of the other groups. Encourage discussion from an "I" position among the groups—avoid "wipe out" arguments.

150

2nd Mod:
Negative
and
Positive
Aspects

The sex act reinforces the attitude and relationship one has with another person. Persons engage in sexual intercourse for many reasons, some of which may be negative and some positive in effect. Placing these in a continuum, a range can be shown from one extreme to another. (You may wish to place a continuum, such as is shown below, on a placard to use with the group.) Explain the items shown. Then ask persons in the group if they wish to add or subtract or rearrange the items, as they examine their own position.

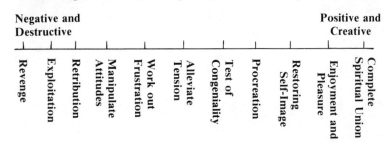

Negative and Destructive — Positive and Creative

Revenge | Exploitation | Retribution | Manipulate Attitudes | Work out Frustration | Alleviate Tension | Test of Congeniality | Procreation | Restoring Self-Image | Enjoyment and Pleasure | Complete Spiritual Union

3rd Mod:
Relational
Insights
The positions taken by the subgroups should remain on the chalkboard, with abbreviated indications of the reasoning for the positions taken. These positions are assumed to have integrity and are not judged by team leaders as being "good" or "bad."

You will want to share with the group some basis for relationship. We work from a relational-intergenerational perspective, and the insights below are principles you may wish to share with the group:

Balanced Ledger. Each person invisibly records his or her feelings of giving and getting in relationship. When the ledger is out of balance, a distorted relationship results.

Systemic Relationships. Loyalties to family of origin, the values and beliefs, as well as the experience of relationship observed between parents affect one's expectations and ability to meet the needs of another. This heritage must be considered in understanding one's sexual responses.

Accountability. One must be accountable and must be willing to hold the other accountable in relationships. This means a willingness to give and an ability to receive in equal measure and to communicate what the felt needs are. Over-giving may in the long run be destructive and fill the partner with guilt. Fairness, trust, and reciprocity are important ingredients of satisfactory relationships.

151

Ask individuals to measure their own values against these and encourage free discussion of how each of the five attitudes toward sex (discussed in 1st Mod) relate to these basic principles.

session 7
remarriage without regret

Reflection

The previous discussions have uncovered many of the factors which make for successful marriage. A review of such factors provides a practical summary of the six sessions that have gone before.

Projection

The objective is to examine the relational areas that need to be probed in remarriage and to consider some of the reasons for failure.

Preparation

Study the material in chapter 7 of the Resource Book. You may wish to interview a marriage-counseling service staff in your community to discuss the primary reasons they have found for failure and success in marriage, particularly in remarriage.

Conducting the Session

1st Mod: Remarriage calls for creative trust which assumes
The Extended the ability to enter into relationships from the
Family integrity and strength of an "I" position. To enter remarriage, a person should be sufficiently self-accepting and self-directional to be a real person to whom others can relate. Both parties must be prepared to work candidly on those areas of relationship that are most apt to distort the second marriage. No area of relationships is neglected more than that of the primary and extended families of each of the partners.

To move from abstractions, arrange for two persons to diagram their family relationships and the way remarriage impinges upon those relationships. One of the persons should be one who is planning for remarriage in the near future, and the other should be one who for the moment is rejecting the possibility of remarriage.

152

These two may be members of the seminar or someone from the outside. Ask each of them to diagram on the chalkboard at least three generations of his or her family. For example: Joe is divorced from Anne, and Joe is planning to marry Sally. Joe and Anne have two children, and Sally (a widow) has one. Joe's father, but not his mother, is living. Both of Anne's parents are living, as are Sally's parents, although they live at a distance. There are brothers and sisters in all the families concerned. You will need to help the selected persons draw the diagram. The following mythical family given here is an example; you will want the persons to draw their actual relationships.

```
 (G F)──(  )  (G F)──(G M)      (  )──(G M)  (G F)──(G M)
  │           │                 │           │
┌─┴──┬─────┬──┴──┬──────┬──┐  ┌─┴──┬────────┴──┬──┐
(  )(JOE)(  )(  )(ANNE)(  )(  ) (  )(  )      (  )(SALLY)
    ┊                 │              │              ┊
    ┊        ┌────────┴───┐         │              ┊
  (JIM)    (BOB)                  (MARY)
    └────────────────────── POSSIBLE   MARRIAGE ────────────┘
```

2nd Mod: **Facing** **Issues**	Ask the group to indicate the specific relationships on the chalkboard which seem most likely to be points of tension in a remarriage. For example: The relation of Joe's children and Sally's children; the relation of Joe's father and Sally's father; Sally's discipline of Joe's children, etc.

153

Ask the "Joe" or "Sally" to share with the group what he or she and the intended mate have done thus far in facing the issues and preparing for them. Let group members enter into the discussion of other points, urging them to share from their own experiences. For the person not intending to remarry, draw out some of the reasons for holding back and show the connection with the basic relationships on the chalkboard.

The leaders should interpret the intergenerational impact of the primary family members (grandparents, parents, siblings, children) and the extended families (uncles, aunts, cousins) on the dynamics of remarriage.

3rd Mod: **Personal** **Application**	If time permits, divide the group into subgroups and let them discuss any of the above considerations applicable to their own situations. They may wish to draw up their own lists of concerns related to their own consideration of remarriage.

session 8
dimensions of a new life

Reflection

Resources needed to support and sustain courageous facing of one's situation have been underscored throughout the sessions. Values, belief systems, and life power are needed for the future.

Projection

The objective is to help individuals become aware of psychic strength and life power available to them through their belief systems, faith, and experiences.

Preparation

154   After reviewing the chapter on "Dimensions of a New Life" in the Resource Book, the leaders should consider the psychic powers they themselves have drawn upon in coping with life and the power that appears to be available to them. Prepare copies of the form "The Experience of Power."

Conducting the Session

1st Mod: Ask the group members to name sources of help
Sources   from beyond themselves which enabled them to
of Help   handle the past experiences. Note that God's power
                 is available from within (psychic power) and from
                 without (as in the case of the Christian family
bearing one another's burdens). When the group is comfortable with the concept of power that has helped them, pass out the form "The Experience of Power" and ask the individuals to list two or three items under each of the four categories. Allow for questions of clarification; the leaders may need to give some examples under the headings. Discuss the meaning of the "natural" inclination to help others that has been present through the centuries; relate this to the strong instinct for survival within the species and present in individual members.

THE EXPERIENCE OF POWER

In my experience of adjusting to life as a single parent, I have found help from other people. These are examples:

Help from Individuals

(Relationship of persons who helped and what they did)

Help from Organizations

(Public and private organizations that helped and how)

I became aware of life power during this experience.

From Within Myself

(Instances where I was stronger than I thought I was)

From Outside Myself

(Power or life force that seemed to be available to me)

2nd Mod: Facing Issues
What are the responses to the pain or suffering of single parents that tend to separate a person from the normal sources of strength? Ask the group to brainstorm on this. Some answers might be:

Friends cut off; I didn't want to talk to them.

Stopped going to religious services; doubted religious beliefs.

Became cynical and suspicious of everybody.

Rejected anything beautiful—no one to share it with—too painful.

The comments might be grouped under categories, such as severing relationships with family; withdrawal from groups and organizations; avoiding personal enrichment.

155

3rd Mod: Looking for Answers
Draw on material in chapter 8 of the Resource Book and your own general experience to describe some of the restless search for meaning and power in life. Then form discussion groups (3 or 4 people) with a resource leader in each to share the meaning and the power they want in their own lives and in the lives of their children. Discourage one person superimposing a way of thinking upon the others.

Ask the groups to report out in plenary session; list the major themes on the chalkboard. Select one or two themes from this discussion and raise the question of how these can be cultivated as a resource in daily life:

How to become better informed

How to develop a disciplined program of personal growth

How to involve the family in awareness of power in life

How to become involved in organized groups (church, synagogue, etc.)

Assess the role of exploring groups, family cluster group,* etc. Other:

Raise the question of how faddism, quacks, con-groups, and exploitation can be recognized and avoided.

Closing the Session

Leaders should express their appreciation to the group for their willingness to share their lives with the others. The group should feel affirmed in this closing session. Many groups decide to continue to meet because of the close ties formed during the intensive sessions; others decide to have a closing social evening in the home of one of the members. Still others project a check-up meeting three or four months hence. In any event, the leaders should speak of their own personal growth during the sessions and their expectations of continuing development in the lives of the group.

---

*Herbert A. Otto, *The Family Cluster: A Multi-Base Alternative* (Beverly Hills, Calif.: The Holistic Press, 1972).

selected bibliography

Ashbrook, James B., *In Human Presence—Hope*. Valley Forge: Judson Press, 1971.

————, *Humanitas*. Nashville: Abingdon Press, 1973.

Bach, George R., and Deutsch, Ronald W., *Pairing*. New York: Avon Books, 1975.

Baer, Jean L., *The Second Wife*. New York: Doubleday & Company, Inc., 1972.

Bel Geddes, Joan, *How to Parent Alone*. New York: The Seabury Press, Inc., 1974.

Bohannan, Paul, ed., *Divorce and After*. New York: Doubleday Anchor Books, 1971.

Boszormenyi-Nagy, Ivan, and Spark, Geraldine M., *Invisible Loyalties*. New York: Harper & Row, Publishers, 1973.

Caine, Lynn, *Widow*. New York: Bantam Books, Inc., 1975.

Chapman, A. H., *The Games Children Play*. New York: Berkley Publishing Corporation, 1972.

Dodson, Fitzhugh, *How to Father*. New York: Signet, imprint of The New American Library Inc., 1975.

————, *How to Parent*. New York: Signet, imprint of The New American Library Inc., 1973.

Dow, Robert Arthur, *Ministry with Single Adults*. Valley Forge: Judson Press, 1977.

Douglas, Williams, *The One Parent Family.* Graded Press, 1971.

Edgren, Harry D., *Fun for the Family.* Grand Rapids, Mich.: Baker Book House, 1975.

Egleson, Jim and Janet, *Parents Without Partners: A Guide for Divorced, Widowed, or Separated Parents.* New York: E. P. Dutton & Co., Inc., 1961.

Gardner, Richard, *The Boys and Girls Book of Divorce.* New York: Jason Aronson, Inc., 1971.

Ginott, Haim G., *Between Parent & Child.* New York: Macmillan, Inc., 1965.

_____, *Between Parent & Teenager.* New York: Macmillan, Inc., 1969.

Gordon, Thomas, *Parent Effectiveness Training.* New York: Peter H. Wyden, Inc., 1970.

Grollman, Earl A., ed., *Explaining Divorce to Children.* Boston: Beacon Press, 1972.

Hunt, Morton, *The World of the Formerly Married.* New York: McGraw-Hill, Inc., 1966.

Krantzler, Mel, *Creative Divorce.* New York: M. Evans & Co., Inc., 1973.

Laing, R. D., *Self and Others.* New York: Penguin Books, 1972.

Maddox, Brenda, *The Half-Parent.* New York: Signet, imprint of The New American Library Inc., 1976.

May, Rollo, *Love and Will.* New York: Dell Publishing Co., Inc., 1974.

O'Neill, Nena, and O'Neill, George, *Shifting Gears.* New York: M. Evans & Co., Inc., 1974.

Sheresky, Norman, and Mannes, Marya, *Uncoupling: The Art of Coming Apart.* New York: Dell Publishing Co., Inc., 1973.

Tournier, Paul, *The Meaning of Persons*. New York: Harper & Row, Publishers, 1957.

⸺, *The Whole Person in a Broken World*. New York: Harper & Row, Publishers, 1964.

Zavala, Ann, *You Can Be a Good Parent on a Low Budget*. Books for Better Living, 1974.